Collector's Encyclopedia of the

DAKOTA POTTERIES

Identification & Values

By Darlene Hurst Dommel

COLLECTOR BOOKS

A Division of Schroeder Publishing Co., Inc.

The current values in this book should be used only as a guide. They are not intended to set prices, which vary from one section of the country to another. Auction prices as well as dealer prices vary greatly and are affected by condition as well as demand. Neither the Author nor the Publisher assumes responsibility for any losses that might be incurred as a result of consulting this guide.

On the cover:

Dickota Badlands swirl vase, $150.00 – 175.00;
Rushmore uranium glaze vase, $125.00 – 150.00;
University of North Dakota Art Deco deer vase, $1,500.00+;
Pine Ridge geometric motif tumbler, $75.00 – 100.00
Messer Hereford figurines, $300.00 – 350.00 each;
Rosemeade pheasant salt and pepper shakers, $25.00 – 35.00.

Cover design by Beth Summers
Book design by Joyce Cherry

Searching For A Publisher?

We are always looking for knowledgeable people considered to be experts within their fields. If you feel that there is a real need for a book on your collectible subject and have a large comprehensive collection contact Collector Books.

ACKNOWLEDGMENTS

This book is dedicated to my husband Jim for his constant support, encouragement, and assistance. Our first piece of Dakota pottery, purchased in 1969 — a University of North Dakota covered wagon vase with a brochure tucked inside — became the catalyst for 26 years of interest in the art potteries of the Dakotas.

I want to thank my children Diann, Christine, and David for patience and understanding on family trips researching and collecting throughout their childhoods. My special thanks to Diann for her advice and computer expertise.

The staff of the State Historical Society of North Dakota, especially Curator of Collections, Mark Halvorson; the staff of the Chester Fritz Library; and Jim Norine provided valuable assistance with resources.

Thanks to Con and Sandy Short, Darlene Martin, and especially Arley and Bonnie Olson for information and pricing assistance.

I am also grateful to Editor Lisa Stroup, the Collector Books staff, and my photographer, Peter Lee, for helping make this writing project a reality.

The wonderful pottery people, whom I interviewed and came to know as friends, made this book possible through generously telling their stories, especially — the late Hildegrade Fried Dreps, the late Howard Lewis, Eunice Messer, Ella Irving, Bernice Talbot, Joe and Betty McLaughlin, the late Freida Hammers Rich, the late Margaret Pachl, the late Bruce Doyle, Jr., John Houser, and William and Peggy Tallman.

We who have lived in Dakota
We who have loved her right well
We who have known her, and tried her,
Marvelous tales could we tell.

Huldah L. Winsted

PREFACE

The Collector's Encyclopedia of the Dakota Potteries is intended as a sampler guide to each pottery, based largely on primary sources and interviews with principals. Photographic examples are representative of the potteries.

Prices, based on mint condition, are only a guide, providing a general overview of scarcity and quality. In some instances, values are difficult to determine as the items are seldom on the market.

Collectors are referred to the bibliographic resources for further information. Appendix I also lists museum sources and Appendix II, a collector's group. Hopefully, this book will stimulate further research, study, and preservation.

CONTENTS

The Song of the Pot

I am a lucky little lump of North Dakota clay,
My heart is filled with gladness
And I sing a song all day,
For a potter found me worthy of his very finest ware,
And fashioned me upon his wheel
With tender loving care.
With the magic of his fingers gave me form and life and soul,
Transformed me from a shapeless clod
Into a flower bowl.
And as I hold within my arms a prairie rose bouquet
I bless the hand that made me
All from North Dakota Clay.

Margaret Kelly Cable

University of North Dakota Pottery

arle J. Babcock, University of North Dakota chemistry instructor, brought the state national fame by recognizing and promoting the potential usefulness of North Dakota clay. An enthusiastic 24-year-old graduate of the University of Minnesota, Babcock "compensated for his lack of technical training by his energy and imagination."[1]

Using buckboard or bicycle, Babcock spent his summers surveying the state mineral resources. After discovering large quantities of native clay, analysis and testing of his collected samples revealed superior quality for pottery-making.

The first publication of Earle Babcock's survey findings was issued in 1892. This bulletin stirred public attention and the legislature responded with pressure on the university for economic development implications. Therefore, the UND School of Mines, which had come into existence in 1890, was finally activated in 1898 with Babcock as director.

Pottery made from North Dakota clay was first displayed at the 1904 St. Louis World's Fair. Dean Babcock had enlisted the assistance of several eastern potteries and the Art Institute of Chicago, sending quantities of North Dakota clay and ordering various types of pottery. The earliest know pottery made at the University of North Dakota are pieces by Marcia Bisbee, UND graduate and chemistry instructor. A bisque leaf ashtray, green glazed ashtray, and two green glazed candlesticks marked "1904" are part of the present UND collection. One or more of them were most likely displayed at the 1904 fair, along with a large collection made into ware by the other potteries. According to a local newspaper, the products "attracted wide attention," and people had difficulty believing that this beautiful pottery was made from North Dakota clay.[2]

The National Corn Exposition in 1909 presented another opportunity for exhibition of North Dakota pottery. By this time, Dean Babcock and Miss Bisbee were teaching a few ceramics classes in the chemistry department. Engineering students had started experimenting with sewer tile, insulators, brick, and other utilitarian wares, which were shown at the Corn Exposition. Babcock also ordered pottery made from North Dakota clay at the Ferock Studio, Zanesville, Ohio, and Minneapolis Handicraft Guild.

In 1910, a Ceramics Department was established through the persuasion of Dean Babcock. At first, ceramic research was the primary purpose of the School of Mines Ceramic Department. Instructional work was soon successfully added. Pottery instruction seemed appropriate for the university curriculum, combining industry, art, and science. Earle Babcock hired Margaret Cable, a Minnesotan from the Handicraft Guild of Minneapolis, to head the newly established department.

Because of their immense impact, a perusal of artists/instructors provides insight into the history and phases of UND pottery.

Margaret Kelly Cable — "the North Dakota poet of the potter's wheel who left UND with an international reputation and a legacy of trailblazing in her field"[3] — became the heart and soul of UND pottery. During her 39 years as ceramic department director from 1910 – 1949, Margaret Cable successfully pioneered the testing of native clay, perfecting of suitable glazes, starting of ceramic classes, and creating of unique pottery.

Margaret Kelly Cable. Ceramics Department photograph, courtesy of the Elwyn B. Robinson Department of Special Collections, University of North Dakota.

Because her family was unable to afford a college education, Margaret Cable became an apprentice in the Handicraft Guild pottery department in 1906. During her four years of practical work and teaching, Cable took several courses, studying design and composition from Ernest A. Batchelder, head of the Batchelder School of Design, Pasadena, California. Margaret Cable sought to constantly further her self-directed education. She studied in summer schools with such master potters as Charles Binns, considered the founder of American Studio pottery, and Frederick H. Rhead, renowned English potter who greatly influenced American ceramics. Several other summers were spent in hands-on training at large commercial potteries in East Liverpool and Zanesville, Ohio, as she broadened her knowledge by working and studying. She also toured several nationally recognized potteries.

Part of Margaret Cable's success appears to stem from the nationwide network she established. She wrote frequently to notable individuals and potteries for their advice and assistance. Cable continued her contacts with Handicraft Guild staff. A long-term professional relationship with Charles Binns began with a 1912 letter and included many correspondences over the years. Several contacts included Arthur E. Baggs, Marblehead Pottery; Stanley Burt, Rookwood Pottery; and Paul Cox, Iowa State College. Just as she was assertive and persistent in seeking advice, Cable's personal papers also indicate a great willingness to help others.[4]

The daughter of a pioneer missionary, Margaret Cable described her successful character traits. "My father's Yankee blood stimulates enthusiasm in my work which is rather of a pioneering character."[5] Her mother was Scotch-Irish. "The Scotch bids me be conservative, helps me stick to a problem and see it

through with patience and perseverance in the face of many difficulties and problems which constantly arise in connection with my work. The Irish helps me to laugh at the failure both in pots and plans, starts me on again for it is hard to squelch an Irish man. He is sure to bob up smiling."[6] Cable's tenacity shines through as she described problems of students making colonial tea sets in 1912. "We have naturally run up against a good many difficulties but you know a good potter never becomes discouraged and we are winning out."[7]

An inspiring teacher, Margaret Cable encouraged her students to explore and develop. As an early student recalled, after Cable instructed on the basics, with students doing hand-thrown and then molded pieces, the students were encouraged to design their own ware.[8] Cable taught about the various potteries of the United States, both commercial tableware potteries and ornamental potteries. She wanted to instruct her students on the history of each pottery, its clays, processes, decorations, and glazes, as well as "the place in the world of commerce or craftsmanship that the finished product occupies."[9]

The 1915 San Francisco Panama Pacific Exposition gave Cable's North Dakota pottery national exposure. Early testing of raw materials at the North Dakota School of Mines and creation of utilitarian products continued during Cable's early years at UND. Utilitarian ware such as jugs, jars, sewer pipe, electrical fixtures, and fireplace tiles filled some of the San Francisco display cases. However, art pottery gradually became the emphasis under Cable's direction. Several imposing exposition cases also displayed decorative but useful ware like vases, tea sets, hair receivers, tobacco jars, and jardinieres, for a total of 208 pieces.

In 1916 the North Dakota School of Mines became the College of Engineering. However, much pottery continued to be marked with the School of Mines seal and many people continued to used the Mines name.

A popular lecturer-demonstrator who became known as the "Lady of the Wheel," Cable displayed her skill and the UND wares at numerous schools, clubs, fairs, and winter shows. UND pieces were also often offered for sale at these educational meetings. Named by Governor A. G. Sorlie as North Dakota's Outstanding Woman in 1927, Margaret Cable demonstrated on the potter's wheel at the Women's World Fair in Chicago. She emphasized not only the excellent North Dakota clay deposits but "that it is a delightful state in which to live."[10]

Demonstrating and lecturing at the 1933 Chicago World's Fair in the North Dakota building gave Cable more national recognition. As she demonstrated, Mar-

Panama Pacific Exposition, San Francisco, 1915. Ceramics Department photograph, courtesy of the Elwyn B. Robinson Department of Special Collections, University of North Dakota.

Women's World Fair, Chicago, 1927, with Margaret Cable. Ceramics Department photograph, courtesy of the Elwyn B. Robinson Department of Special Collections, University of North Dakota.

garet Cable's desire was to "grasp and hold the imagination."[11] Bertha Palmer praised her success, "While Miss Cable throws the clay and fashions it with her skillful fingers as we watch, she describes and shows to the fascinated watchers the different stages through which the clay and vase must pass before it becomes the thing of beauty which everyone who sees covets."[12]

Her personal correspondence indicates a politically savvy Margaret Cable, who sent Christmas greetings to various state officials in the form of UND pottery. Several of these officials, including a U.S. Senator, then continued to order the pottery. Presentation pieces were also ordered for visiting dignitaries.

Perhaps Margaret Cable's joy, enthusiasm, and love for making pottery are best expressed in her poem "Song of the Pot." Cable viewed herself as part of a long tradition, often citing this Biblical quotation, "And the Lord said to Jeremiah, as clay is in the potter's hand so are ye in my hands, O house of Israel."[13] She defined pottery as "truly creative art, in it there is a blending of the artist, the craftsman, and the technician."[14]

In 1915, Margaret Cable attained national recognition by being awarded the highest honor in ceramics, the Charles Fergus Binns medal of the American Ceramics Society for "High Achievement in the Field of Ceramic Art." Margaret Cable retired and moved to Los Angeles, California, in 1949, where she died in 1960.

Hildegarde Fried, who was in Margaret Cable's first 1910 class, graduated from UND in 1913. After working as a high school principal, Fried studied ceramics at UND and became a part-time student assistant. Fried became the first faculty addition when she was hired by the UND Ceramics Department in 1918. Her bachelor's degree in chemistry and mathematics helped her assume a dual role of researcher and teacher. Fried described her tenure at UND as doing "experimental work with the different types of glazes that were suitable to the different types of clay in our state. Much of my time was spent in the laboratory making up a great variety of glazes and testing them on the pottery, as well as assisting in the classroom."[15]

In the summer of 1918, Hildegarde Fried and Margaret Cable attended an eight-week summer session at the New York State School of Ceramics, Alfred, New York. With Charles Binns as instructor, "We spent most of our time there at the potter's wheel and doing experimental work in different types of glazes."[16] Binns' book, *The Potter's Craft*, was the textbook used in most college ceramics courses across the country, including UND. The two women continued on to visit several factories, including Marblehead Pottery, Marblehead, Massachusetts, and Lenox Inc. in New Jersey.

The daughter of a pioneer who served two terms in the North Dakota House of Representatives, Hildegarde Fried loved to travel. An August 9, 1922, postcard to Margaret Cable pictures Anton Lang, well-known German potter. Fried attended the Oberammergan Passion play, in which Anton Lang played the role of Christ. Hildegarde told of being entertained in Lang's home several times and purchasing 13 pieces of his pottery.

Hildegarde Fried.

After her 1924 marriage to Dr. Joseph A. Dreps, another faculty member, Hildegarde Fried Dreps resigned from UND, having contributed much to UND as student, faculty member, and house mother of Delta Gamma, her own sorority.

Moving with her husband to college towns in Nebraska and Missouri, Hildegarde completed her master's degree in psychology and art and displayed her work in college exhibits. She traveled extensively with Dr. Dreps, a foreign language professor. Writing and lecturing became creative endeavors. Hildegarde had a book, *Oars in Silver Water*, published, as well as 45 articles and over 100 poems in magazines. Even at age 85, she continued to submit her writing, listing her number of publications "so far."[17]

Hildegarde's home in the 1970s reflected her creative life and strong arts and crafts influence. The walls were covered with her oils and watercolors. A complete set of her handmade wicker furniture furnished one room. Besides her ceramics, other Dreps works included the media of brass, copper, aluminum, plastic, and wood. Hildegarde Fried Dreps died in Maryville, Missouri, in 1977.

Flora Cable Huckfield, at UND 1924 – 1949, joined her sister Margaret Cable at UND after her husband's death. As assistant in the ceramics department, according to former dean Milton B. Larson, Mrs. Huckfield did not teach.[18] Primarily a gifted decorator, she soon took charge of the wares made for sale. By 1930, Mrs. Huckfield was no longer on the university faculty list or payroll, as pottery sales paid for her salary.

Dean Larson described Flora Huckfield as a "pleasant person who was very meticulous in her work." [19] John Howard, student assistant from 1936 to 1937, gives us a further glimpse of Huckfield's ability, stating that she was an expert at applying sprayed glazes, sitting for hours in her little glazing booth.[20] Many quality UND items bear the name "HUCK" and a student's name. These pieces were evidently handthrown by students and then decorated by Huckfield. Carefully inscribed marks, indicating HUCK, the design name, and year, often appear. Huckfield also often worked on special orders, souvenirs, and convention items. Since another instructor, Freida Hammers, indicated that Margaret Cable created most of the designs executed by Huckfield, it is difficult to determine how many and which designs originated with Huckfield.

Flora Huckfield and her sister, Margaret Cable enjoyed a close sibling relationship, at UND and their Lake Bemidji vacation cottage. When Margaret Cable retired and moved to California in 1949, Flora Huckfield moved with her, where she died in 1960.

As a successful instructor with 39 years of tenure (1924 – 1963), Julia Edna Mattson also appears to be the most prolific UND artist. After Mattson served as a part-time student assistant in ceramics, Margaret Cable, when recommending her upon graduation for a faculty position, described her as being an agreeable member of the staff with considerable experience, a very hard and efficient worker.

John Howard, student assistant, stated that the students crowded Julia Mattson's classes in her specialty, coil-built pottery. "Miss Cable rather scoffed at building as a way of making pottery, but Miss Mattson stuck to her guns and created some beautiful designs."[21] Clay was rolled in long, spaghetti-like strings, which were then wound round and round to build a pot. A Ceramic Department Open House invitation described hand-coiled pots decorated with Native American symbols.

Julia Mattson's specialty at UND became western designs, especially covered wagons and cowboys. She is also known for her expert use of Native American designs and methods, having studied at the Taos, New Mexico, School of Arts and University of New Mexico. Her master's degree thesis at UND expressed this interest, "A Survey of Indian Pottery, Arts and Crafts and Symbolism, West of the Mississippi River." Besides teaching, Mattson traveled throughout the state and midwest lecturing and demonstrating pottery making. Travels around the United States and Europe inspired her work in ceramics, water color, and oil.

Julia Mattson received many honors. Her work was extensively exhibited, including three large ceramic North Dakota scenic plaques at the 1933 Chicago World's Fair. She was invited to submit her pottery for the Ceramic National Exhibition, Syracuse Museum of Fine Arts, Syracuse, New York. Because the Ceramic Nationals had become a focal point for national recognition in the ceramics field, American ceramists eagerly sought inclusion in the exhibitions. In 1957, Julia was presented a citation of merit for her original work in ceramics and successful teaching by the American Artists Professional League. President John F. Kennedy was presented a Mattson vase at his 1963 Grand Forks visit.

The cobalt blue seal, after fifty years of use as the major mark of UND pottery, was discontinued in 1963 with Julia Mattson's retirement. She moved to Los Angeles and died in 1967.

Freida Louise Hammers, a ceramic chemist at UND from 1926 to 1939, directed testing and experimentation, formulating unique UND clay mixtures and glazes as a research assistant, instructor, and assistant professor. An intelligent young woman, Hammers finished the grades in seven years, high school in three years, and college in three years, graduating Phi Beta Kappa with a B.S. degree in chemistry and physics in 1923, followed by an M.S. chemistry degree in 1925. While a ceramics student at UND, Hammers' scientific training and technical skills were already recognized. After joining the UND department, Hammers studied with Paul Cox at Iowa State College and Glen Lukens at the University of Southern California.

Freida Hammers did not do much teaching. She stated, "My work was mainly in making and developing

Instructors/artists: Flora Huckfield, two unidentified men, Freida Hammers, one unidentified man, Julia Mattson, and Margaret Cable, according to Freida Hammers Rich. Ceramics Department photograph, courtesy of the Elwyn B. Robinson Department of Special Collections, University of North Dakota.

glazes, working out new clay bodies, making plaster-of-paris molds, working out firing curves, and supervising firing."[22] With meticulous records, experimentation at UND flourished during Hammers' era.

Also, "endowed with artistic talent,"[23] Freida Hammers described her own decorative work as sgraffito or incised, often with naturalistic bands. But she stated that "more and more as time went on, the pieces I made were used to test glazes."[24]

Margaret Cable perceived Freida Hammers as a "splendid technician as a potter and decorator, with practical training and skills in potting, her artistic talents, together with her earnestness of purpose, her record of quiet efficient service and her pleasing personality all combine to make her a highly desirable member of the ceramics department."

UND was a beloved family institution for Freida Hammers. Her mother, campus nurse and later supervisor of UND dorms, took ceramics classes for three years, signing EMH for Elsie Marie Hammers. Her sister, Clara Tussing Ingvalson, also took ceramics classes at UND.

Health problems forced Hammers to resign from UND in 1939. She became an analytical chemist for the University of Minnesota Soils Department in 1942, where she worked until 1954. In 1954, Hammers married Merton C. Rich. Freida Hammers Rich died April 7, 1977, in Yucaipa, California, where she had moved in 1972.

A product of the progressive Alfred University with its emphasis on individuality and artistic freedom, Margaret Davis Pachl came to UND, upon Margaret Cable's retirement in 1949. After receiving both her bachelor and master of fine arts degrees from Alfred, Margaret Pachl directed the Kalamazoo, Michigan, Institute of Fine Arts Ceramics Department. Her summer education included ceramic sculpture with Alexander Archipenko, Woodstock, New York, and drawing with Boardman Robinson, Colorado Springs Fine Arts Center. Study with California artist Marguerite Wildenhain stressed hand craftsmanship. Seminars with England's Bernard Leach and Japan's Shoji Hamada emphasized international styles and utilitarian aspects. Pachl's educational background motivated her to revolutionize the UND Ceramics Department as Assistant Professor of Ceramics.

Drawing upon her own varied background, Pachl promoted broad diversity in her students, her goal being "to help students develop their own abilities and be creative."[25] Her modernistic designs were considered by some to be "heavy, crude, raw, and clumsy," and created conflict with other UND faculty members, like Julia Mattson.[26] However, a former student described the pottery work, under Pachl's tutelage, as "much more broadly creative and expressive."[27] Works of Margaret Pachl were honored for exhibition at the Ceramic Nationals, Syracuse Museum of Fine Arts in 1948 and 1953. Several other shows and exhibitions at museums across the country also included Pachl's creative efforts.

When Margaret Pachl resigned in 1970 after 21 years at UND, she was teaching over 100 students a term. The college, acknowledging the difficulty of replacement, began to look for someone with a "strong orientation toward the practical aspects of ceramic art and its development."[28]

Margaret Pachl moved to Eureka Springs, Arkansas, where she continued to produce creative pottery. In 1978, a picturesque setting of wooded hilly areas surrounded her studio/home, perched on a hillside slope and stilts. She sold her work through the Eureka Springs Arts, Crafts, and Handicraft Shop. As her health failed, Margaret Pachl's pottery-making diminished until she died in 1982.

The continuously evolving art styles of UND pottery reflect the UND artist/instructors — their training, philosophies, and times.

Prior to Margaret Cable's tenure at UND, utilitarian ware was the major pottery component. Cable soon introduced art pottery, created for decorative purposes, as the focus.

Margaret Cable was a product of the Minneapolis Handicraft Guild with its arts and crafts emphasis on hand craftsmanship, structure, and simplicity in form and decoration. Cable learned not only arts and crafts skills, but also its ideals and values. In her writings, she often expressed the ideals of art, beauty, and utility combined. The tenets of the Arts and Crafts Movement were spread through teaching. Cable's adult classes, which started a year after she came to UND, are a good illustration of the arts and crafts concept of community outreach.

Margaret Cable and Hildegarde Fried, UND's first instructors, soon progressed onward as they studied at Alfred University and other potteries. Both Cable and Fried were students of Charles Binns. As Binns encouraged potters to develop their own individual paths by studying past

Margaret Pachl at the wheel. Ceramics Department photograph, courtesy of the Elwyn B. Robinson Department of Special Collections, University of North Dakota.

Classroom instruction, December 5, 1923. Ceramics Department photograph, courtesy of the Elwyn B. Robinson Department of Special Collections, University of North Dakota.

historical styles, Cable and Fried appear to have done this at UND.

The influence of their visits to china factories can be seen in products Fried and Cable made when they returned to UND. Many tea sets, cups and saucers, plates, bean jars, and other tableware were produced, using an opaque glaze perfected by Fried. Hildegarde described the diverse ware of her era, "decorations on the raw or fired ware were put on under the glaze or over the glaze. Different colored glazes, often green or blue, were airbrushed on, sprayed on, or the piece was dipped in a jar of glaze. Sometimes a salt glaze was also used. We carved designs onto the clay and used different stencils to produce patterns. Some pieces were fired three times depending upon the decorations and glazes."[29]

Already in 1915, Cable sought Japanese stencils to use for decorating art pottery. Designs desired included birds, cherry tree boughs, chrysanthemum, and clusters of grapes and leaves. The Japanese influence is shown occasionally in UND in various time periods.

In 1918, Margaret Cable wrote to several companies seeking "decalcomania patterns in conventional designs suitable for use on a cream colored body."[30] Cable's interest in conventional designs reflected the Handicraft Guild influence, expressed by Judson Webb.[31] She wanted strong dark colors, like blues or browns and especially single motif or medallion designs used for borders. Borders of this type, used extensively by Dedham Pottery, were very popular at the time. A Handicraft Guild artist reminisced making "borders of rabbit, rabbit, rabbit" on metal, pottery, and cloth.[32] Cable's request for decal designs suitable for water pitchers, steins, and tea tiles indicates utilitarian products being made at UND.

Early UND pieces mimicked the muted matte glazes and conventionalized geometric patterns of Marblehead, which Cable considered "the most artistic pottery produced in this country today." Border scenes and mottos characteristic of Saturday Evening Girls pottery appeared. The typical forms of Newcomb, airbrush graduations of Rookwood, and organic shapes of Teco all surfaced in early UND.

Influences of Art Nouveau and Art Deco, popular stylistic movements of the time, appear on UND pottery. Art Nouveau, a richly ornamental style, emphasized curving flowing lines to realistically depict organic qualities. The subsequent Art Deco period turned to streamlined, functional, abstract design, often reducing form to geometric shapes.[33]

Much of the early UND art pottery was made from white clay. According to Hildegarde Fried, this clay was so free of iron and manganese, it could be used without added ingredients. Cable described using "an

Early pottery. Ceramics Department photograph, courtesy of the Elwyn B. Robinson Department of Special Collections, University of North Dakota.

exceptional high grade clay which burns to a soft ivory tint" to make "ivory-colored tableware similar in color and quality to famous Royal Doulton."[34]

While early UND pottery reflected past and current styles, new directions gradually emerged. UND did not attain national recognition by adhering to the styles of other potteries. Margaret Cable obviously observed distinctive regionalism, like the sailing motifs of Marblehead Pottery, reflecting its fishing village origin, and Newcomb College, with its extensive use of Louisiana imagery such as oak trees draped in Spanish moss. As Margaret Cable interpreted her own world and turned to the prairie for inspiration, she created truly unique pottery.

By 1927, prairie motifs were being used "to make this pottery wholly indigenous to North Dakota."[35] According to Margaret Cable, "wheat, our chief agricultural product, stands first in favor, followed closely by the cowboy, the buffalo, the coyote, and the Indian."[36]

Wildflowers were an obvious choice for UND designs as they can still be found in all parts of the state, with a vast variety of over 1,250 known species.[37] The wild prairie rose, state flower of North Dakota, was one of several native flowers used frequently. Another, the pasque flower, its pale lavender blooms abundantly covering undisturbed prairie, is a harbinger of spring. The state flower of South Dakota, the pasque flower was often used as a UND design, gracing the matching Cable bowl and vase presented to Queen Marie of Rumania by Governor A.G. Sorlie. Other popular flower motifs were the blue flax and the red field lily "which 'toils not' but lifts its flaming face to the sweep of the sky which is Dakota."[38]

The meadowlark, "whose liquid note will soon herald the coming of spring is a favorite bird."[39] The clear flute-like song of this gregarious bird echoes across the prairie landscape. Chosen not only as the state bird of North Dakota, but also for such states as Montana, Wyoming, Nebraska, and Oregon, the meadowlark became one of UND's best-loved designs.

The flickertail, North Dakota's state animal, was "used in never-ending variations."[40] South Dakota's state animal, the coyote, whose long melancholy wail reaches across the prairie, was another favorite motif. The covered wagon and Red River oxcart were other native designs.

The North Dakota Products Vase, made from native clay by Margaret Cable for Governor A.G. Sorlie at his request, is an outstanding example of the indigenous UND concept. Decorations symbolized state agricultural and industrial development. Two livestock panels include pig, cow, and sheep figures. Poultry industry motifs appear on a third panel, with a fourth highlighting the milling industry. Hardy winter wheat separates the panels. Honey bees buzz around the mouth of the vase, while a base ornamental band includes a potato, sugar beet, prairie rose, and North Dakota's mineral

resources — lumps of lignite coal and clay.

Margaret Cable had already started the North Dakota emphasis when Julia Mattson joined the faculty. Mattson expanded the breadth of design production with her western and Native American motifs and even some hokey themes, like "Why Not Minot?"

Characteristic 1927 UND glazes used on a 23 piece exhibit for the national meeting of the American Ceramic Society are described by Margaret Cable. "The matt glaze is characterized by a dull metallic sheen in russet brown, fir green, cloud gray, huckleberry green, or orange. The gloss glaze is of fine texture, brilliant surface, and soft pastel colors, the charm of which lies chiefly in its blended effect. A delicate rose shades into lavender suggestive of a dove's breast; or a celadon green loses itself in a hyacinth blue."[41]

Freida Hammers, with her technical background, sparked striking glaze changes. One of Hammers' first assignments as a UND staff member was to develop a lower-fired, warmer-colored clay body. Over the years, various native clay combinations were used until a satisfactory four clay mixture evolved in 1938, which was then used extensively. Brighter gloss glazes, like Rooster Red, Hepatica Blue, and Pepperberry also emerged.

The use of bentonite clay to develop "Bentonite Finish" became a UND specialty for which Freida Hammers is recognized. Early in her efforts, Hammers described the new glaze as an "interesting medium of expression which will produce unique effects at a much lower cost than with any glaze we could use."[42] Bentonite clay was effective as a glaze, but could not be used alone as its tendency to swell when wet caused stickiness and extremely high shrinkage.

Hammers' experiments with this readily accessible North Dakota product produced a burnt sienna red as well as cream, yellow, dark brown, and black. With iron in bentonite causing colors, addition of expensive colorants was not necessary. However, the bentonite could also be mixed with mineral colors "to obtain interesting and colorful decorative effects."[43] Direct application to the bisque ware, requiring only one firing, was another cost advantage.

Bentonite flowed evenly from the brush, forming a smooth glaze, free of crazing, with an almost iridescent sheen. This glaze proved to be especially well-suited for Native American and western motif pottery. Presentation pieces, including a 1939 buffalo design vase for Crown Princess Martha of Norway, utilized Freida Hammers' bentonite glaze.

Hammers stated that during her years at UND most pieces were molded, the molds being made by students and faculty. Occasional pieces were thrown by Margaret Cable or Julia Mattson.

UND ceramics classes remained very popular for years, filling to capacity with long waiting lists. In afternoons, special adult classes were conducted. These students included university presidents' wives, faculty

Bentonite pottery. Ceramics Department photograph, courtesy of the Elwyn B. Robinson Department of Special Collections, University of North Dakota.

wives, and townspeople. According to Freida Hammers, regular and adult special students were usually taught first to construct pieces by coiling and slabs. Slab pottery is fashioned by cutting flat thin pieces, much like cutting fabric for a dress pattern, and then fitting the pieces together. For coil pots, long molded clay coils are wound. Then, the students learned how to use the potter's wheel, design pieces, make molds, execute designs, and spray glazes. Charles Binns' *The Potters Craft* continued as the textbook.

Pottery made entirely from easily available North Dakota materials with simple, low-cost equipment was a UND concept developed in the mid-30s and named "Prairie Pottery."[44] This project furthered arts and crafts values, with pottery method instructions prepared for schools and club projects. Prairie School architecture was a popular Midwestern regional style, described by architect Irving Pond as "echoing the spirit of the prairies of the great middle West."[45] Whether this movement influenced Cable's terminology is unknown.

Margaret Cable signed some of these prairie pottery pieces "Maggie Mud," a nickname. The name "Prairie Pottery" was used again in 1940 for less than a year. A promotion of American Designs, Inc. of New York attempted to influence American design through the collaboration of designers and manufacturers. Again, Cable signed her submitted pieces "Maggie Mud."

Per a 1927 suggestion by Ralph Budd, Great Northern Railroad Company President, Glacier National Park souvenirs were made by UND and sold at park hotels. Other souvenir requests from commercial enterprises, community organizations, and the college soon followed. UND commercial ventures expanded into thousands of paperweights, trays, plaques, nut cups, curtain pulls, medallions, and other souvenirs.

Freida Hammers Rich described her creation of a buffalo nickel replica made as a traveling trophy for the winning University of North Dakota/North Dakota State University homecoming game. Later, a Native American to represent UND (the Sioux) and a buffalo to represent NDSU (the Bison) were made as medallions. These medallions, about the size of a silver dollar, were worn around the neck and sold for a quarter as team souvenirs. The medallions were punched out in quantity using a mechanical press.[46]

Margaret Pachl brought different art biases. Freeform, modern-style art influences of the contemporary studio potter predominated during her era.

Margaret Cable discovered the secret for the great desirability of UND pottery. "This colorful ware, made from local clays, decorated with the plant and animal forms indigenous to the state seems literally to breathe the spirit of the pioneer and the prairie."[47]

From the beginning, North Dakotans were eager to

purchase UND pottery and sales of UND give indications of quantities produced. Early on, some pieces were sold at annual department exhibitions. Other sales were made at state capitol exhibitions when Margaret Cable gave illustrated talks to women's groups. As Cable states in a 1918 letter, "we do not make a practice of selling our wares but do so only as an accommodation to those who are interested enough in them to write in for them or come after them."[48]

As demand for UND pottery became "more and more insistent,"[49] orders for such things as fireplace tiles, lamp bases, and vases were filled. In a 1926 letter, Cable described the current sales method as a laboratory shelf, known as "the pottery sales shelf." She requested greater sales opportunities, asking to place pottery for sale "in a few of the larger cities of the state" instead of just restricting sales to buyers making "direct personal contact with the ceramic department."[50] UND pottery was then placed in shops, mainly within North Dakota and also some other states.

In 1938, a traveling salesman, A.E. Spencer was hired on commission. Selling to gift shops, drug, jewelry, and department stores in North and South Dakota, Minnesota, Iowa, and Nebraska, Spencer enjoyed brisk UND sales. By 1952, UND pottery had "found its way into every state in the union and many foreign countries."[51]

The school was able to produce pottery comparable in quality and character to that of commercial pottery operations. From the beginning, UND used investigative methods, operational processes, and standard machinery like that of ceramics industries.

With the retirement of Margaret Cable and Flora Huckfield in 1949, pottery was no longer produced "on a large scale for sale purposes."[52] The decline of public sales and changing pottery styles away from naturalistic prairie motifs at UND brought diminished public interest.

UND was nationally recognized early as quality pottery. An American Pottery exhibition by the General Federation of Women's Clubs with "sixty pieces from the best potteries in our country" included Newcomb, Marblehead, Pewabic, Overbeck, Rookwood, Paul Revere, Van Briggle, Teco, Dedham, Fulper, and North Dakota School of Mines.[53]

An art critic, after systematically observing ceramic art at the 1933 Chicago World's Fair, reported the outstanding examples as being from Sweden, UND, Japan, and American Indian. "The outstanding exhibit of United States pottery comes from a state little known to the world for its ceramic products. At the University of North Dakota, Miss Margaret Cable has developed a ceramics

department and a type of pottery of great interest."[54]

For 50 years from 1913 to 1963, a cobalt blue University seal was used to mark most UND pottery. Even though the UND School of Mines became the College of Engineering in 1916, the School of Mines seal continued to be used until 1963. Mark emphasis is explained by Margaret Cable, "Each piece bears the stamp of the University on its base applied under the glaze in cobalt blue, the most indestructible color of the potter. This means that as long as a fragment of the seal remains the color of the printing will be as legible as it was the day it came from the kiln, and will still proclaim to all the world the worth and value of North Dakota clay."[55] Some early pieces or pieces too small for the seal were stamped or hand-printed "UND" or "U.N.D. Grand Forks, N.D." After 1963, items were only marked with the students' names.

Most UND is signed by the artist. However, a name signed on the bottom of a piece does not necessarily mean that person created the design. As Freida Hammers stated of one design, "We made many wheat-design vases this way, using Miss Cable's pattern."[56]

Some UND pieces are dated. Dating can also be accomplished by several other means — tenure of instructors who signed pieces, use of white clay during the early years, and a design numbering system detailed in the Barr, Miller, and Barr book.[57]

Although Hildegarde Fried described hammering of inferior quality pieces, imperfect pieces were sometimes sold as seconds during Hammers' time. For example, a crazed or leaking piece might be sealed by pouring varnish inside and then sold as a second.

As quality of UND varies significantly, the merit of each piece must be judged individually. Instructor/artists generally created the highest-quality, most-valuable UND pottery. However, some student pieces are exceptions.

Many fine examples of UND pottery may be viewed in the two collections on the University of North Dakota campus at the Hughes Fine Arts Center and the J. Lloyd Stone Alumni Center. (Appendix I)

UND has enjoyed popularity because of its superior quality and appeal to those who live close to nature in their everyday lives. Native flora, fauna, and themes have provided design material that brought joy and created unique pottery. The flowers, birds and beasts which inhabit North Dakota offer wide interest. The scenes depicted by UND artists are also part of our natural heritage. Today, collectors respond to these motifs as did buyers of yesteryear.

Round cobalt seal used from 1913 to 1963.

Variation with "M. Cable" on seal.

Handled 8" Ferock, pre-UND vase, made in Ohio from North Dakota clay $500.00 –
850.00; two-color Ferock 2½" x 7¼" bowl, marked "FEROCK 43 ND," $1,250.00+.

Early 4" pitcher incised "UND 1911," with the glaze and shape showing Minneapolis Handicraft Guild influences, $200.00 – 250.00.

Utilitarian 3½" x 7¼" bowl, $150.00 – 200.00.

Mark on early utilitarian products.

Early pieces made by Hildegarde Fried from white clay. Blue 2¼" x 3¾" soup bowl and 5½" saucer with silver rims, $175.00 – 200.00; white 4" tumbler with blue flowing glaze, $150.00 – 200.00; blue shaded 2½" egg cup, made in 1924, $125.00 – 150.00; experimental 5½" tile, $200.00 – 225.00; aqua 3" matte glaze vase, $75 – 100.00; blue shaded miniature 3" vase, $75.00 – 100.00; green gloss 3½" vase with ruffled top, $75.00 – 100.00.

White clay 2¼" x 4½" pitcher with blue stencil, marked "U.N.D." by hand in blue ink, $200.00 – 250.00.

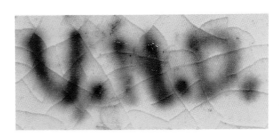

Early mark.

Tea set, 4½" teapot and 2½" sugar/creamer with decal designs on ivory, $500.00 – $750.00. (Courtesy of State Historical Society of North Dakota.)

Back left to right: bowl 3½" x 6¼" airbrush shaded matte glaze, purple to blue, made by Hildegarde Fried at Alfred University, signed "H. Fried A.U.," $200.00 – 250.00; 3¼" vase made by Hildegarde Fried in 1920 at UND with similar shaded purple glaze, $200.00 – 250.00; 4½" shaded matte green to mauve vase made by Fried at Alfred University, marked "HF 18," $250.00 – 300.00; front: 1½" x 4¾" mahogany matte bowl made by Fried at UND with North Dakota clay, $225.00 – 250.00; covered 1½" x 4¾" mahogany matte bowl made by Fried at Alfred University, $225.00 – $250.00.

Bean pot, 5½" x 5", shaded green to blue and marked "H Fried Feb 12-24," $350.00 – 400.00. This bean pot and a poem were given as a gift from Hildegarde Fried to her fiance, Joseph Dreps, who loved baked beans.

Yellow 3" x 6" bowl of white clay by Hildegarde Fried, $200.00 – 250.00. Few yellow glaze pieces appear to have been made in the early years. Student assistant John Howard stated that Margaret Cable preferred students not use yellow because Dean Earle Babcock didn't like the color.

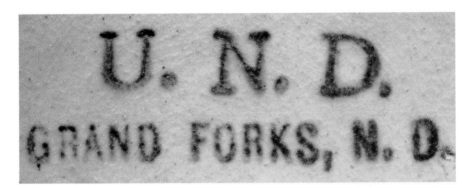

Ink stamp mark.

Art Nouveau 6½" x 7" plaque by Hildegarde Fried, $1,500.00+.

21

Stylized Julia Mattson candleholders, 7½" high, base 5½" wide, $2,000.00+ pair. (Courtesy of Steve Schoneck collection.)

Lavender 4¼" vase with slip-painted purple flowers by Huckfield, reminiscent of Rookwood's Iris line, $400.00 – 500.00; sgraffito floral 3¾" vase, marked "HUCK 599 Rose," $450.00 – 500.00; blue shaded to green gloss glaze 9¾" vase given as a wedding gift to Hildegarde Fried by "HUCKFIELD 1924," $400.00 – 500.00; 3" bowl with slip-painting, marked "Ottem-HUCK 4683," $400.00 – 500.00.

Glazes by Freida Hammers Rich. Green metallic glaze 6" vase, $400.00 – 450.00; green gloss shaded glaze on 4½" vase, $300.00 – 350.00; shaded rust to midnight blue matte 5½" vase, $225.00 – $250.00.

Art Deco 8" sgraffito vase with scene depicting deer, flowers, and meadow, artist signed and dated "M. Cable 1946," $1,500.00+.

Florals by Cable. Blue gloss 5" pitcher with tulip designs, $350.00 – 400.00; bowl 3" x 6" with "PASQUE FLOWER," $400.00 – $500.00; prairie rose 2½" vase, $250.00 – 300.00.

Group shows wide range of Julia Mattson's ware. Modernistic 6" cone woman, $150.00 – 200.00; Viking ship in relief on 2¾" vase, $350.00 – 400.00; blue gloss 5" bud vase with wild roses, $200.00 – 250.00.

Sgraffito 3" x 6½" bowl with incised mark "LEWIS-328-HUCKFIELD," $400.00 – 500.00. (Courtesy of State Historical Society of North Dakota.)

Huckfield 2½" x 5" bowl marked "Prairie Rose," $250.00 – 300.00; sgraffito mules 3¾" x 5¾" bowl by Mattson, $400.00 – 500.00; Mattson 2" x 5" green metallic glaze footed bowl, $250.00 – 300.00.

3¾" x 5¾" bowl, colors described by Margaret Cable as "delicate rose shades into lavender suggestive of a dove's breast," signed by Mattson and Huckfield, $150.00 – 200.00.

Prairie Pottery 2" x 7¼" bowl with Native American motifs, signed with Margaret Cable's nickname, "Maggie Mud," $400.00 – 500.00.

Mark of bowl.

Meadowlark 3" x 3¾" bowl incised "M. CABLE MEAD-OWLARK 155," $400.00 – 500.00; brown Huckfield incised wheat 2½" vase, $150.00 – 175.00; 4⅓" honey pot with bee finial, $250.00 – 300.00; blue matte Huckfield 1¼" x 6½" bowl with green wheat spray brushed with metallic brown, $275.00 – 325.00.

Blue 3¾" x 6¼" bowl with wheat sgraffito design, $350.00 – 400.00.

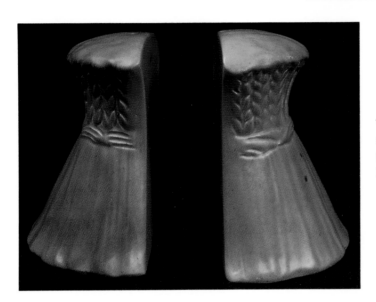

Wheat shocks 5½" bookends in matte maroon glaze by Margaret Cable, $450.00 – 500.00. (Courtesy of State Historical Society of North Dakota.)

Wheat shocks in relief and slip-painted 4½" vase by Huckfield, and "ICH," $375.00 – $425.00.

Vase 3½" matte rust background with brown slip-painted coyotes circling, by Julia Mattson, $450.00 – 500.00.

Sgraffito 3½" coyote vase of rust with cobalt blue design, also by Mattson, $450.00 – 500.00. (Courtesy of State Historical Society of North Dakota.)

Western motifs. Covered wagon 3½" vase with incised design by "WHITE-HUCK 2069," $400.00 – 500.00; sgraffito 7" vase of cowboy roping bronco by Julia Mattson, $500.00 – 600.00; oxcart 1½" x 4½" ashtray, marked "M. CABLE RED RIVER OX CART 174," $250.00 – 300.00; white oxcart 4½" pitcher by Margaret Cable, $300.00 – 350.00.

Huckfield 5" hanging plaque of oxen pulling covered wagon, $250.00 – 300.00. (Courtesy of State Historical Society of North Dakota.)

Bucking broncos matte brown 7" vase, signed "MATTSON 1938 COWBOY," $500.00 – 600.00. (Courtesy of State Historical Society of North Dakota.)

Mattson 6" horse; 2¼" Mattson dog; 2¾" peasant girl signed "Morax"; 3" x 5" pelican by Mattson; 2" Mattson lion; 3¼" Mattson terrier. $200.00 – 300.00 each.

Bentonite glazes. Native American motif 2½" x 4" vase with bird design, artist-signed "Eul-land," $400.00 – 500.00; Mattson 3" x 3½" vase with Native American motifs of deer, marked "PRAIRIE POTTERY U.N.D. GRAND FORKS JM 64," $1,000.00+.

Bentonite 4¼" x 5" bowl with Native American motifs, signed "EYAMOED 39," $400.00 – 500.00.

Rare nude 5" bookends by Julia Mattson, $500.00 – 750.00.

2¼" prairie rose vase, signed "CABLE 759," $250.00 – 300.00; prairie rose ashtray 3½" with "H 3792," $150.00 – 200.00; pink 2½" x 4½" bowl with geometric band design, marked "HUCK 3437," $300.00 – 325.00.

Floral 5½" pitcher, signed by Margaret Cable and Julia Mattson, $300.00 – 350.00; prairie rose 2¾" sugar and 3½" creamer by Margaret Cable in 1944, $150.00 – 200.00; tulip salt and pepper shakers, $50.00 – 75.00; 5½" pitcher, signed "JARVIS," $200.00 – 250.00.

Cherry blossom slip-painted 7½" ginger jar with oriental influence, thought to be a graduation gift to Freida Hammers from Margaret Cable, $2,000.00+.

Marks on ginger jar.

Pin tray, 3½" with flickertail and wheat design by Mattson for the "Tolley, N. DAK GOLD-EN JUBILEE," her home town, $75.00 – 125.00; 6" fish ashtray marked "UND Flossie MC," Flossie being Flora Huckfield's nickname, $100.00 – 150.00; Laura Taylor 5" tray, $75.00 – 125.00.

Madonna 6" figurine by Mattson dated "JUNE 1942," $300.00 – 350.00. (Courtesy of State Historical Society of North Dakota.)

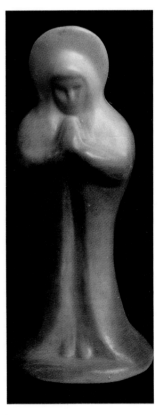

Curtain pulls, 1½" to 2½", $75.00 – 150.00 each. Flickertail with wheat; prairie rose; Sakakawea, a Shoshone Native American woman who guided the Lewis and Clark expedition; flower design; pasque flower.

2¼" medallions symbolizing North Dakota football teams, $75.00 – 100.00. The Native American chief symbolizes the Sioux of the University of North Dakota, the Bison is the mascot of the North Dakota State University.

American Legion 17th annual convention 2½" medallion, $100.00 – 125.00; blue 2" medallion for Home Economics department in 1945, $75.00 – 100.00; 3½" Astor Medal replica for Columbia River Historical Expedition, $350.00 – 500.00; Norwegian Dancers 2" medallion for Daughters of Norway, 1939, $75.00 – 100.00; gold and blue 2½" medallion "P.T.A. MOTHER SINGERS," $50.00 – 75.00.

Rebekah Assemblies 3¼" blue paperweight, $50.00 – 75.00; blue coyote 3" paperweight for North Dakota Rainbow Assembly, $75.00 – 125.00; white 2½" coyote paperweight, $75.00 – 125.00; wine 3" coyote paperweight, $75.00 – 125.00; Walter L. Stockwell 1933 Masonic 5" x 3" plaque with hanger, $75.00 – 100.00; Parents Day metallic green prairie rose 3½" paperweight, $75.00 – 100.00.

4-H club 3½" paperweight, $75.00 – 125.00.

Pin trays. 3¾" maroon gloss covered wagon; 3¼" Mattson prairie rose; 4" Native American chief, creme with tan highlights; 3¾" deer and trees in relief; 3½" Mattson tan. $150.00 – 200.00 each.

Simple shapes of beginning students. Slab landscape 2¼" x 3¾" box, $50.00 – 75.00; 4½" reticulated candleholder, $25.00 – 35.00; hand-molded 2½" vase, $10.00 – 15.00; 2¼" pencil holder, $5.00 – 10.00; hand-molded 3½" dish, $10.00 – 15.00.

More intricate pieces composed by UND students. Asbtract design on reticulated 4" vase, signed "AMUNDSON," $75.00 – 125.00; 3" flower frog, "AXTEL," $50.00 – $75.00; bowl, 2¾" x 3¾" with fish, "AMUNDSON," $100.00 – 150.00; green metallic glaze 4" horse by Ruth Rudser in 1932, $100.00 – 150.00; 4" paper doll cowboy motif vase for children, dated and signed "5-30-57 Hanson," $350.00 – 450.00.

Covered 4" x 6½" bowl with applied rose, "JARVIS," $200.00 – 250.00; black matte glaze with relief rose design highlighted by gold 4¼" x 6¼" vase, signed Huckfield and "A SORBO 196" $300.00 – 350.00; 3½" x 4½" fish bookends, marked "3-21-1944 Haesle 177 MC," $300.00 – 350.00.

Metallic black glaze 6½" vase with incised flowers, "CUSHMAN," $300.00 – 350.00; 3" rose gloss glaze bowl with slip-painted cobalt blue floral design, "Tollefson 1949," $300.00 – 350.00; 5½" x 6" vase, shaded blue to rose, "ELSIE PETERSON," $150.00 – 200.00.

Low dish, 1¼" x 5", with incised beaver motif and signs indicating "BEA" and "ME," signed "Lebacken," $200.00 – 250.00.

UND pottery by Margaret Pachl, signed "pachl" or "mp." Tan 6½" vase, $75.00 – 100.00; gray 2" x 4½" bowl, $25.00 – 35.00; chartreuse 3¼" x 5¼" bowl, $30.00 – 50.00; brown 4" vase with small opening, $35.00 – 50.00; covered 5½" container, $50.00 – 75.00; brown 2½" vase with green paper seal, $30.00 – 50.00; gloss glaze gray and green 5½" pitcher, $75.00 – 100.00.

Green paper seal.

UND Pachl jug, 5½", $75.00 –100.00.

Mark of Pachl's studio pottery.

Crystalline glaze 3½" vase made by Margaret Pachl in her Eureka Springs, Arkansas, studio after leaving UND, $75.00 – 100.00.

Experimental marks.

Lamp bases. 8" gloss green, $250.00 – 300.00; 12½" airbrush shaded glaze by Freida Hammers, $300.00 – 350.00; 8¾" matte brown, $200.00 – 250.00.

Fraudulent 4¼" x 4½" very heavy piece of tan with black, incised "ELM."

Mark of fraudulent piece, reading "NORTH DAKOTA SCHOOL OF MINDS."

The following inserts were taken from *"Pottery from North Dakota Clays."*

N THE SOUTHWESTERN PART of North Dakota there are extensive deposits of high grade pottery clays. Some of these clays are of unusual purity. In their natural state they have a composition very similar to many of the artificially prepared clay bodies, which have been built up to the proper composition in the pottery, often by the mixing of several materials.

An abundant supply of fuel is essential to the development of a clay industry. North Dakota is particularly fortunate in having extensive deposits of lignite closely associated with the higher grade clays. Lignite is now used successfully for burning clay products.

THE PRESENCE and potential value of the clays of North Dakota were first called to public attention by the late Dr. Earle J. Babcock, Dean of the Engineering Colleges of the State University, in a bulletin published in 1892. Realizing the importance of these clays in the economic development of the state, he spent many years in investigation in the field and laboratory. In 1910 the Ceramic Department of the School of Mines was established. In this department it has been possible, not only to make chemical analyses and physical tests, but also to actually make up the various types of finished products for which the clays are adapted, thus proving out their use and value in a practical way.

An important function of the department is the testing of raw materials for structural and utilitarian products such as brick, tile, sewer pipe, jugs, cooking wares.

IN ADDITION, some of the purer clays fitted for the more exacting and decorative products are made up into pottery and ivory bodied table wares.

Science, industry and art are coordinated in the ceramic industry, which attains its highest expression only when scientific knowledge coupled with skillful technique, is guided by artistic design. It is appropriate therefore that the making of artistic pottery be emphasized.

The demand for this pottery has been so insistent that a limited part of the ware produced in the normal operation of the department is sold. In this way the legitimate longing to possess a piece of this truly distinctive ware is satisfied; at the same time the superior quality of the various clays used is proven out in a thorough manner on a large scale.

"Turn, turn, my wheel'
Turn round and round
Without a pause, without a
sound:
So spins the flying world
away!
This clay, well mixed with
marl and sand,
Follows the motion of my
hand;
For some must follow, and
some command,
Though all are made of
clay! —LONGFELLOW

POTTERY as made from North Dakota clay is frequently fashioned on the potter's wheel, a method known as "throwing." A ball of plastic clay is thrown down on the surface of a horizontal revolving disc or wheel. By pressing the clay with both hands the ball is forced into a cone shape in the exact center of the wheel. By inserting one thumb in the top a round symmetrical opening is formed. The fingers of one hand enlarge this opening by pressing against its inner surface while the other hand steadies and squeezes the clay on the outside. The clay, seeking relief from the pressure, rises upward taller and thinner, forming the walls of the vessel.

Artists have delighted in the potter's wheel since the ancient Egyptians and Greeks threw graceful forms upon its rhythmic surface.

CLAY FORMS can be quickly made and duplicated by a method known as "casting" in plaster of Paris molds.

A creamy mixture of clay and water termed a "slip" is poured into the mold, which, being dry and porous, absorbs the water in the slip in contact with its inner surface, stiffening it into a wall of clay called a cast. The thickness of the cast depends upon the length of time the slip stands in the mold. When the cast is of the proper thickness the mold is inverted and the surplus slip is poured out. This leaves the vessel hollow.

When the cast is thoroughly dry it is given the first firing in a potter's furnace or kiln; the once fired ware known as "biscuit" is now ready for this application of the glaze.

THE BISCUIT WARE is covered with a thin layer of glaze sprayed on by compressed air. Two or more colored glazes are frequently sprayed on the same pot, the result being an exquisite imperceptible blending of color. After glazing, the pieces are fired to an intense white heat which melts the raw glaze into a thin glassy covering.

North Dakota pottery is finished in either matt or gloss glaze. The matt glaze is characterized by a dull metallic sheen in russet brown, fir green, cloud grey, huckleberry blue or orange. The gloss glaze is of fine texture, brilliant surface and soft pastel colors, the charm of which lies chiefly in blended effects; a delicate rose shading into lavender suggestive of a dove's breast; or a celadon green which loses itself in a hyacinth blue.

THE DECORATED WARES are of two types, those with designs carved in low relief upon the surface of the damp clay vessels and those with patterns painted in mineral pigments or colored glazes upon the biscuit ware.

To make this pottery wholly indigenous to North Dakota, in addition to fashioning it from native clays, design motifs are drawn from the prairie. Native flowers, plants, birds and animals are therefore used; the wild rose, our state flower; the pasque flower; the blue flax; the golden wheat; the red field lily which "toils not" but lifts its flaming face to the sweep of sky which is Dakota; the meadow lark, nature's first heralder of spring; the flickertail, the Indian and the buffalo—these and many more constitute a wealth of design material peculiar to the prairies.

Each piece of North Dakota pottery is marked on the bottom under the glaze in indestructible cobalt blue with the seal here shown.

THUS out of the experimental and research work of the School of Mines there has been developed in the Ceramics Department, a pottery ware made from native clays, which is technically excellent and artistically pleasing; a ware of which North Dakota may well be proud.

Dickota Pottery

Clods of clay— too long
you've lain awaiting
the potter's hand.
You're destined now to
please the eyes of
men throughout the
land.

Your gorgeous hues of
reds and blues
Of tans and buffs and
creams,
Are truly those the
potters choose
To weave in many
themes.

Tis "Dickota" I shall
name this ware
From which these clays
have come.
And shape the clay with
gentle care
As the potter's wheel is
spun.

C. Grantier

Dickinson Clay Products Company — Dickota Pottery

Colorful swirls, blended matte hues, mottled pastel glazes, western designs — all describe Dickota pottery. With its trade name formed from the first four letters of the manufacturing city, Dickinson, and the last three letters of the state, North Dakota, this beautiful pottery grew out of an old brickyard.

The Dickinson Fire and Pressed Brick Company was founded in 1892 by Dr. M.A. Brannon, later president of the University of North Dakota and W.S. Russell. Dean Earle J. Babcock, cited earlier as instrumental in establishing the University of North Dakota School of Mines, provided counsel for the new enterprise. The brickyards continued until 1934. Then, after reorganization, Dickinson Clay Products Company became the new company name.

Howard Lewis, with his creative innovation and expertise, opened new horizons for the old brickyard after being hired as plant superintendent in 1935. As a ceramic engineering student at Iowa State College, Lewis had studied with Paul Cox, well-known ceramic chemist who created Newcomb College's famous soft matte glaze. Paul Cox enabled Lewis to complete his college education by hiring him as a student to rebuild their kiln and develop Iowa clay deposits. Lewis was the only member of his ceramic class to get a job upon college graduation in 1932. At the Niloak Pottery Company, Benton, Arkansas, Lewis developed new glazes and clay mixtures for the Hywood line. A periodical of the time described him as a persistent hard worker, who "prefers the practical application of his knowledge on a commercial scale to the pursuit of theory,"[1] a preference demonstrated repeatedly in his life.

Howard Lewis came to the North Dakota brickyard as "they wanted to make glazed brick."[2] Lewis was soon directing research, experimenting with local clay deposits and glazes. Lewis discovered that the North Dakota clay was suitable for making good pottery.

Although the brickyards produced tile for such major projects as the new state capitol being constructed in Bismarck, the brickyard couldn't operate during the cold winter months and had to close down. Howard Lewis started pottery production to give the brickyard workers indoor winter work, keeping the

Howard Lewis. Courtesy of Marian Dommel.

plant running all year, instead of on a seasonal basis. New machinery and equipment were purchased and workers trained.

Native clay from western North Dakota was used. The University of North Dakota had provided earlier successful experiments on this clay, defining the properties making it well-suited for pottery making. Bentonite, another plentiful North Dakota clay product, was mixed with this earlier clay "to add to its permanency and its water shedding properties."[3]

When Charles Grantier, a native North Dakotan, joined the company in 1935, he brought experience in the use of North Dakota clay. Having previously studied with Margaret Cable as a student at the University of North Dakota, where he became student assistant in the ceramics department, Grantier was "familiar with all the possibilities of North Dakota clay when used for the manufacture of pottery."[4] Most importantly, Grantier, as designer, brought his western spirit and inspiration to the company. Already in 1935, Grantier's design of a small buffalo, promoting North Dakota on the pedestal, had become popular. Grantier's unique teepee incense burner also reflected western characteristics.

The popular motif, "Sundogs," depicts rainbow-like lines radiating toward the sun near the horizon. In this design, Charles Grantier was reflecting upon the beautiful natural phenomenon of this area, as sundogs appear in vivid display in cold Northern winter climates. The bright, luminous rings, which appear to the right and left of the sun, at the same elevation above the horizon, are caused "when the sun shines through airborne ice crystals."[5] A company brochure describes the motif as "typifying the rising of the sun over the Badlands,"[6] a somewhat different meaning than actual sundogs. A low-relief, running border of the pattern was used with several shapes and colors. As recognized art pottery historian Marion Nelson notes in *Art Pottery of the Midwest,* the design becomes more pronounced when covered with several glazes that separate over the relief design.[7]

Besides his ceramics achievements, Charles Grantier also became a master handweaving hobbyist, a skill learned during his long isolated winters as a country school teacher. Grantier was named outstanding North Dakota artist in 1953. Among Grantier's other artwork awards was a 1954 national citation from the American Artists Professional League.

Margaret Cable, Director of the Ceramics Department at the University of North Dakota, came to work at Dickinson Clay Products in the summer of 1936. According to Howard Lewis, she designed dinnerware which became known as "Cableware." This line is characterized by concentric rings as seen in a wheel-thrown teapot, signed "M. Cable 1936." Production of the dinnerware continued after Margaret Cable returned to the college. Documentation of other ware designed by Cable, besides the dinnerware, has been difficult to establish.

According to a letter of Howard Lewis, "Laura Taylor came to Dickinson for a few months to conduct pottery classes for the WPA and she also helped us for a short time."[8] Laura Taylor, previously a student of the University of North Dakota, became Director of the North Dakota Works Progress Administration Ceramics Project and later was to play a significant role in the development of the North Dakota ceramics industry as co-founder of the Wahpeton Pottery Company.

Sam Zook, general manager and a ceramic engineer himself, in August, 1935, described the pottery production as a project initiated as a side line, which was projected to soon outstrip the brickmaking as a business producer. Zook commented further, "We can meet any kind of legitimate competition, both as to price and quality and beauty of product."[9] As Zook predicted, the pottery production soon outpaced brickmaking and the company became know for its art pottery.

Retail sales started in Dickinson. The ware was then introduced in Mandan and Bismarck, later being distributed in the Midwest, especially in North Dakota, South Dakota, and Minnesota.

"Dickota Badlands," the company's best-known pottery, was named for the natural grandeur of southwestern North Dakota. Steep canyons, towering spires and rugged hills created a colorful painted landscape of haunting shapes and shades, the Badlands. Red, blue, green, brown, gray and creamy-white clays, reminiscent of the subtle landscape coloration, are swirled together on the potter's wheel to create Dickota Badlands pottery. Comparing the colors in a Dickota example to swirl ware of other potteries, Marion Nelson refers to Dickota as having "greater brilliance than those in most Arkansas examples, but they are just as harmoniously blended."[10]

Howard Lewis, who brought the technique to Dickota, had learned to make swirl pottery while at Niloak Pottery, Benton, Arkansas. However, he stated repeatedly that he worked mainly with the Hywood line at Niloak and did not make swirl ware while there. He learned the swirl process by watching Charles D. Hyten, Niloak's creative owner. The potter starts with white clay, and adds oxides — cobalt blue for blue, ferric oxide for red, chromic oxide for gray, copper oxide for green, iron oxide for brown, and tin oxide for white. The potter then pulls slabs of the colored clay together, cuts the layers and throws the mixture on the wheel. Stripes are formed as the pottery is pulled up. Mixing clays for swirl is a difficult procedure as the various colored clays tend to shrink and separate after firing. "Colors must also be carefully planned in relationship to each other for harmony and appearance."[11]

Much of the ware is covered with glazes using an airbrush to blend colors, a technique then commonly used at the University of North Dakota and several other potteries. Laura Fry of Rookwood Pottery had first "introduced the use of color in delicate graduations through the use of a mouth atomizer" in 1884.[12] The airbrush was later developed for this technique. Lewis had used this technique at other potteries, including Broadmoor of Denver, Colorado.

Mottled glazes of pastels and white were effectively used on various shapes. Howard Lewis stated that he learned this technique when he worked at a Chicago terra-cotta plant between stints in college. The air pressure on glazing-spray guns was cut down so gobs of glaze were thrown out onto the vases. A 1932 newspaper article mentions Lewis's earlier experiments "with a mottled matte glaze in soft tones of green and blue for a new line of clay pottery"[13] already when he was at Niloak.

The company also made large quantities of commercial ware, especially ashtrays, used for advertising. Examples include an order for 15,000 horseshoe-shaped ashtrays for a North Dakota creamery. Another, for the Lewis and Clark Hotel, depicts Chief Red Cloud, a Native American warrior, who also appears on state highway markers.

Legal problems resulted when the pottery produced a water pitcher similar to a glass one made by a glass company. The pottery mold was made by shaping clay over the glass pitcher. After Dickinson Clay Products received a letter from attorneys, stating that the glass company held the shape patent, Dickota stopped making the item. Although some attribute the plant closing to legal difficulties, Howard Lewis did not agree and cited other economic reasons as the cause of demise.

When the old brickyard went broke, the Dickota pottery portion was also forced to close in November, 1937, since it was combined in the same company. However, a stock of inventory remained and Howard Lewis stayed on several months until the pottery was sold out.

The word "Dickota" was scratched on the bottom of most pieces, using a stylus. "Dakota Badlands" was scratched onto the bottom of pieces in this line, often with the initials "HL" for Howard Lewis. Silver or gold paper labels read "Dickota Dickinson, No. Dakota." Some pieces remained unmarked and can be identified by glaze, shape, and clay.

As mentioned, some techniques and shapes of Dickota had been used at other potteries. Ellsworth Woodward of Newcomb Pottery stated, "In the shape of vases it is not possible to avoid imitation, the best forms having been for centuries established."[14]

According to Martin Eidelberg, noted art historian, at the turn of the century American ceramists "not only admired but also imitated their European colleagues' works. This is not to say that Americans needed a specific prototype for each new model they created. Quite the contrary, once there was an initial impetus to move in this direction, nature provided gifted ceramists with an unlimited repertoire of ideas.[15]....Our histories are intertwined and mutually illuminating."[16]

So also, the Dickota ceramists used proven techniques and shapes and then moved forward in their creative endeavors. Such use has not proven to be a detriment for collectors of Dickota in its era or today.

Certain glazes were more sought after, already at time of production. For example, the black glaze is specifically described as coveted in the *Dickota Glaze Book* at the University of North Dakota archives.[17]

Some Dickota manifests a western orientation and theme. Therefore, this pottery appeals not only to North Dakota pottery collectors, but also to collectors of western memorabilia.

As quality pottery, Dickinson Clay Products ware is equally sought by collectors of Dakota and swirl pottery. With its distinctive swirled colors, Dickota Badlands is popular, having been recognized as the company's "finest product from both a technical and aesthetic standpoint."[18]

Dickinson Clay Products Company — Dickota Pottery Marks

Mountain sheep, 4½" x 4¼", bookends, created by Charles Grantier illustrate solid sculptural lines, $400.00 – 500.00.

Mountain sheep bookends in green, showing results of less crisp molds, $350.00 – 450.00 set.

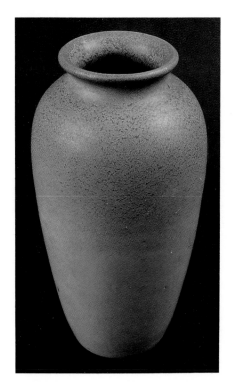

Matte yellow 7" vase with blue sprayed thinly over top, $65.00 – 85.00. (Courtesy of State Historical Society of North Dakota.)

Miniature animals. 2" dog with paper label; 1½" hippo with incised mark; $75.00 – 100.00 each. Limited figurine shapes included prairie dog, elephant, horse, and another dog shape. Some of these shapes also appear to have been used by the Broadmoor Pottery Company.

Salt and pepper shakers. 2" black glossy, $25.00 – 45.00; and 1½" x 2½" maroon red Cableware design, $25.00 – 45.00.

Marine blue glaze with white flowing overglaze. 4¼" ashtray, $35.00 – 45.00; and 4"
vase, $60.00 – 80.00.

Sea green glaze shell dishes, 1½" x 7¼", $25.00 – 35.00.

Sundogs relief border. Orange gloss 4" ashtray $35.00 – 45.00; black gloss 1¾" x 8½" fruit or bulb bowl, $65.00 – 85.00; orange gloss 1¾" x 8¼" fruit or bulb bowl, $65.00 – 85.00; brown gloss 3" x 6½" flower bowl, $65.00 – 85.00.

Close-up of Sundogs motif.

Bright orange gloss glaze with gold/black overglaze. 4" vase, $45.00 – 60.00; 2¼" sugar
and creamer, $35.00 – 50.00; 4¼" vase, $45.00 – 60.00.

Pine Green 3" x 6" vase of high fire glaze, which breaks into patterns when highly
fired, $35.00 – 50.00; and airbrush blended yellow to blue 7" vase, $50.00 – 65.00.

"Dickota Badlands" swirl vases, 6" vase, signed HL for Howard Lewis; 3" vase; 4" vase; 4½" vase. $125.00 – 175.00 each.

Mark showing "Dickota Badlands" and HL.

Shaded matte yellow with blue 3" sugar and creamer, $35.00 – 55.00. (Courtesy of State Historical Society of North Dakota.)

Hanging baskets. 7½" glossy black, $65.00 – 85.00; and 5¼" matte gold with molded decoration, $75.00 – 100.00.

This blue mottled glaze produced by spotting blue matte with white matte and called Peacock Blue, outsold all other glazes, according to the *Dickota Glaze Book*. 4½" x 8" teapot, $100.00 – 125.00; four 4" water tumblers and 8" ice water pitcher, $150.00 – 225.00; Cableware 3½" x 5" bowl, $30.00 – 40.00; 6½" bud vase, $25.00 – 35.00.

Peacock Pink mottled glaze. 7½" vase $65.00 – 85.00; 6½" bud vase, $25.00 – 35.00; 5" water pitcher, $50.00 – 65.00; 2½" sugar and creamer, $35.00 – 55.00; 10" handled vase, $65.00 – 85.00.

Gloss green glaze with metallic sheen on 8" ice water pitcher and six 4" water tumblers, $250.00 – 300.00. This is the pitcher shaped like that made previously by a glass company.

Shield-shaped 2¾" paper-weight, $35.00 – 45.00.

Cableware. Black gloss glaze 3¾" teapot made by Margaret Cable at the Dickinson Clay Products Company in 1936, $150.00 – 200.00; black gloss 1" x 3½" dish, $20.00 – 35.00; 1¾" blue sugar and 2½" creamer, $25.00 – 35.00. The 6¼" x 6½" pitcher made by Margaret Cable and Laura Taylor at UND, was perhaps a precursor of Cableware. $175.00 – 200.00.

Mark on teapot made by Margaret Cable.

8" Cableware plate, $25.00 – $35.00.

Mark on Cableware plate.

Blue handled 5" vase, $40.00 – 55.00; matte blue 2½" What Not Pot $25.00 – 35.00; matching gloss green What Not Pot, $25.00 – 35.00; green 4" vase, $25.00 – 35.00; 6½" green bud vase with drip darker green, $35.00 – 45.00.

Brown Federal Housing 4½" paperweight, $35.00 – 50.00; 4¾" Little Brown Jug, $40.00 – 60.00; blue Federal Housing 4½" paperweight, $35.00 – 50.00.

Cowboy hat ashtrays. On the right, green 4½" x 5" hat promoting Minot, $40.00 – 65.00; on the left, brown 4½" x 5" hat with "NORTH DAKOTA," $40.00 – 65.00. The center hat is unmarked underneath, lighter in weight, and larger than those made by the Dickinson Clay Products Company. This hat was made by a Dickinson sewer pipe company as a promotion in the 1960s, $20.00 – 25.00.

Mark on bottom of Dickinson Clay Products Company hat.

Advertising ashtrays. 5" dark green gloss for Valker Christensen Co.; 4½" gloss blue for the Sherman Hotel; 3¼" whitish aqua for the Koffee Kup; 3" green horseshoe for the Mandan Creamery and Produce Co. $25.00 – 45.00 each.

Brown gloss Chief Sitting Bull 3¼" ashtray, $50.00 – 75.00. (Courtesy of Bill Vasicek collection.)

Ashtray 3¼" described as Badlands in Dickota Pottery sales brochure, $35.00 – 45.00. Instead of colored clay being turned on the wheel to make swirl pottery, this ashtray appears to be molded and then painted. The inside is glazed.

Swirl ashtray mark.

Glazes of pink matte over-sprayed with blue matte. 4" vase made by Broadmoor Pottery, $45.00 – 65.00; 5" Sky Blue Pink vase marked "DICKOTA," $30.00 – 50.00. Howard Lewis worked at Broadmoor before coming to Dickinson Clay Products Company.

Metallic black gloss glaze. 4¾" vase marked "DICKOTA," $40.00 – 60.00; 2¼" Niloak Hywood line bowl, $20.00 – 30.00. Howard Lewis worked on the Hywood line at Niloak Pottery before going to Dickinson.

UND pieces made by Charles Grantier while a student. Cream 5" vase with slip-painted floral design, $75.00 – 100.00; blue 2½" vase with white sgraffito cube decoration, $70.00 – 90.00; hand modeled 5¼" tile with holly motif, $200.00 – 225.00; blue gloss glaze 4½" mug with sgraffito design of "UND" and initial "G" under handle, dated 1932, $200.00 – 300.00.

UND 3¼" x 5" plaque of Italy, made by Charles Graniter, $250.00 – 350.00.

Booklet — *The Story of Dickota Pottery*
(Courtesy of Rita Carew.)

DICKOTA POTTERY

*Clods of clay—too long you've lain awaiting
    the potter's hand.
You're destined now to please the eyes of
    men throughout the land*

*Your gorgeous hues of reds and blues
    Of tans and buffs and creams,
Are truly those the potters choose
    To weave in many themes.*

*Tis "Dickota" I shall name this ware
    From which these clays have come.
And shape the clay with gentle care
    As the potter's wheel is spun.*

C. GRANTIER, 1936.

DICKOTA

Many thousand years this clay lay waiting. Already the finest material of its kind for the production of a fine art pottery, it needed but the touch of the potter's hand to change these humble clods to pieces of enduring beauty. It was not until the Spring of 1935 that a serious endeavor was made to commercialize these vast resources.

In March, 1935, Mr. Howard Lewis, a ceramic engineer, came to Dickinson to direct the research resulting in the ware known as Dickota Pottery.

The first pieces of pottery showed great promise toward further development. From this time on, the work went forward rapidly. The Badlands, sunrises, sunsets, and all our picturesque west furnished a challenge to create a product characteristic of this locality. During the summer Charles Grantier, a westerner in spirit and inspiration, joined the staff in the capacity of ceramic artist and designer.

Shapes bearing the subtle colorations of the Badlands have emerged from our kilns. "Dickota Badlands" is a product of the potter's wheel, being made of clays bearing the blues, reds, grays and cream white colors of the region from which the name is derived. "Sundogs," a unique decoration typifying the rising of the sun over the Badlands, is another of the beautiful patterns now available in several shapes.

Here we see pottery, most ancient of crafts, springing up as a new industry of the State of North Dakota. These clays, the finest in the world, lie readily accessible at the earth's surface. The pottery manufactured is of excellent grade, capable of holding its place in any market; but of particular interest to residents of North Dakota. The industry is now in its infancy—but, *Watch "DICKOTA" Grow!"*

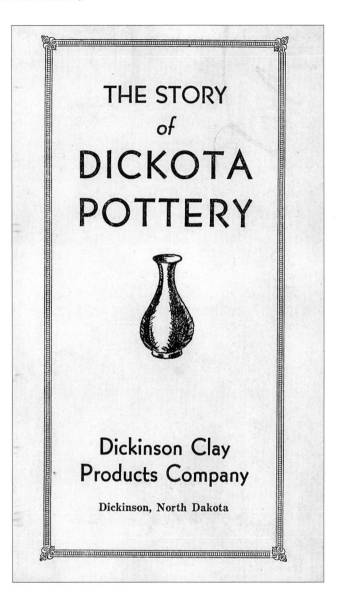

THE STORY
of
DICKOTA
POTTERY

Dickinson Clay
Products Company

Dickinson, North Dakota

*No handicraftsman's art
Can to our art compare;
We potters make our pots
Of what we potters are.*
LONGFELLOW.

Little Boy Blue

Little Boy Blue,
Come blow your horn!
The sheep's in the meadow,
The cow's in the corn.

WPA Ceramics

Out of the Great Depression, which plunged this country into unemployment and despair, grew playful, light-hearted creations as well as utilitarian objects — WPA ceramics.

The plight of needy artists was especially severe during the Depression as their unemployment rate was even higher than that of the general population.[1] As a solution, President Franklin Roosevelt proposed his New Deal federal programs, including a social and economic program, the Works Progress Administration (WPA).

One branch of the WPA, the Federal Arts Project (FAP), was aimed at helping professional artists, training nonartists to make a living working with ceramics, and providing crafts instruction in communities. This program was also seen as a way to keep art from "disappearing in a time of crisis" and an "opportunity to make art accessible to all levels of American society."[2]

Professor William Budge, director of ceramic engineering at UND, was instrumental in bringing WPA to North Dakota. In 1936 Budge, WPA state-wide project director, appointed Laura Taylor state supervisor of the North Dakota WPA/FAP, headquartered first in Dickinson and later in Mandan. A 1936 local newspaper described the five-months old ceramics project as "out of a melee of clay, plaster of paris molds, manicure tools, and ingenuity, come rows and rows of vases, pitchers, bowls, novelties, and 'what have you' through the efforts of twelve WPA employees."[3] Although all eleven staff women had little or no clay work experience, the article stated that several "have displayed unusual ability in designing and modeling, one having been already employed part time at the Dickinson Clay Products Company. Its object, to train otherwise unemployed individuals to earn their own livelihood and to discover hidden talent, has been more than fulfilled." The sole male employee dug and transported the clay. Afternoon classes in modeling were also offered, "with ten women of the city now being instructed by Miss Taylor."[4]

In 1939, Taylor started promoting WPA with wheel demonstrations at the New York World's Fair. When Laura Taylor left North Dakota for New York, she recommended another artist synonymous with North Dakota WPA, Charles Grantier, as temporary state supervisor. Grantier soon became permanent supervisor as Taylor met R.J. Hughes at the Fair and the two of them founded the Wahpeton Pottery Company.

Charles Grantier, a UND graduate with an art major and ceramics minor, had worked as a UND student assistant in ceramics. In 1935, Grantier became a designer for Dickota pottery. Bringing this education and experience to WPA, Grantier, known by his nickname "Happy," expanded production until as many as 18 were employed. Charles Grantier directed the North Dakota WPA until 1942, when the relief operation was no longer needed and the country geared up for war.

Charles Grantier. Courtesy of Arley and Bonnie Olson.

The University of North Dakota had a great influence on the success of WPA in North Dakota. When the project was first set up, Margaret Cable provided advice and loaned equipment, including a potter's wheel. During the early years, all pottery was fired at the Dickinson Clay Products Company, Fort Yates, or UND. Because the local Mandan clay used by WPA was not compatible with glaze formulas originally provided by UND, Freida Hammers and Margaret Cable tested the clays and experimented to formulate new glazes.[5] As Charles Grantier acknowledged in a 1940 letter to Cable after installing WPA's own kiln, "the tender child you nursed as an infant WPA has taken strength from your guidance and can now for the first time try its feet, as a project complete in its own right and under one roof."[6]

Tony Lanz was one of the WPA artists creating hand thrown pottery on the wheel. Margaret Cable, in a letter to Charles Grantier, anticipated a visit from Tony

Lanz to UND, "judging by the Mandan project pots you sent in for firing last summer, I won't be able to show Mr. Lanz any new tricks. They are very nicely done." Lanz went on to work at Rosemeade and his signature appears on some Rushmore pottery.

Correspondence with former UND instructor Freida Hammers Rich indicated that there were also WPA workers at UND. Freida wrote of one man, Mr. Lindholm, who had learned to use the potter's wheel during his youth in Sweden. "All his pieces were hand-thrown. He was good at it and Miss Cable sometimes helped him with the design of a piece."[7] Although Rich stated that Mr. Lindholm's pieces were marked with an "L" preceding the number, it is unknown whether "WPA" appeared on the pieces. Other WPA workers weighed and made up glazes, prepared clays, watched the kiln, and did odd jobs. Freida also recalled two women workers who made molded pieces.

UND records indicate WPA glazes ranging from matte to high gloss and a wide spectrum of colors — orange, brown, and green matte; gunmetal green; semi-transparent blue enamel; and green, blue, and "Pepperberry Red" gloss enamel. Clear colorless glazes were used by themselves to provide a natural clay-colored finish, as well as over sgraffito designs and inside pieces.

WPA products were molded, hand built, or hand thrown in wide variety for state institutions, like schools, hospitals, and libraries. Cookie jars, covered jugs, fruit bowls, incense burners, and vases were all thrown on the potter's wheel. Sgraffito or incised decorated pieces included lamps, vases, candleholders, and bookends. Native American motifs were used on some items. Schools with WPA hot lunch programs and WPA nursery schools, the forerunners of this generation's Head Start program, became the recipients of utilitarian pieces like pitchers, mugs, fruit cups, and cereal bowls. Clear glaze was used for custard cups, being lead-free and, therefore, safe for baking. Other functional WPA products include ashtrays, trivets, spoon holders, flower pots, plates, paperweights, tumblers, juice glasses, salt and pepper shakers, sugar and creamers, mixing bowls, teapots, and trays. Plaques depicting scenes of historical interest were supplied to libraries. A transportation series included an oxcart, covered wagon, and stagecoach. Even some swirl was made at WPA, an influence of Dickinson Clay Products Company, where Charles Grantier had worked and learned the process.

Nursery rhymes enjoyed early pottery popularity. Already before 1916, the Roseville Pottery Company, Roseville, Ohio, illustrated the appeal of nursery rhyme products. The Roseville Juvenile line included Little Bo Peep, Tom the Piper's Son, and Little Jack Horner.[8]

Nursery rhyme figures had been an early WPA focus in other parts of the country. In 1933 – 34 former Cowan Pottery artist, Edris Eckhardt, particpating in a Cleveland pilot program of the Public Works Art Project, conceived the idea of a Mother Goose series of figurines for educational use in libraries.[9] Eckhardt's pragmatic direction was a success as the figurines were ordered from across the country. Soon her department was able to purchase its own kiln and become self-sufficient instead of relying on public school resources. During her term as director of the Cleveland WPA ceramic sculpture department from 1935 to 1941, Edris Eckhardt also supervised limited edition ceramic production of story book characters by other artists. Eckhardt's popular Alice in Wonderland series led to more nursery rhyme figures as well as other characters from children's literature for a total of over 130 designs, including 50 by Eckhardt herself.[10] Pottery characters like Alice in Wonderland were also produced by the Missouri WPA for state nursery schools. However, the Missouri project was soon abandoned because the ware was too heavy and cumbersome.[11]

Laura Taylor initiated the nursery rhyme series at North Dakota, with designs of Humpty Dumpty, Old King Cole, The Fiddlers Three, Mother Hubbard, Peter Peter Pumpkin Eater, and others. Charles Grantier continued the popular figures from beloved children's tales, such as Mary Had a Little Lamb, Three Little Pigs, and Little Red Riding Hood for distribution to state nursery schools as teaching aides.[12] A former watch repairman G. L. Patterson executed the figues during this era. In addition to the nursery rhymes, WPA figures included deer, beaver, polar bear, rooster, dog, horse, buffalo, elephant, lion, turtle, squirrel, and coyote.

A rubber ink stamp, "WPA CERAMICS N. DAK." used to mark most items, remains in the UND collection. Other marks were hand etched or incised. A round seal in blue and black resembles the UND seal. Artists' initials or names also sometimes appear. Some pieces were not marked. Those, marked only WPA without state designation, are also difficult to attribute to North Dakota WPA.

WPA ware has become collectible for several reasons. Historical significance is foremost as many Americans like to collect their history. WPA is part of this nation's saga — a program people remember or have studied in United States history.

WPA nursery rhyme figures are particularly collectible. Nursery rhymes have enchanted their readers for hundreds of years. Even before being written down, these traditional folk verses, riddles, and songs were passed from generation to generation. Although originally crafted for adults, later adaptations created appeal for children. Interest in nursery rhyme memorabilia will continue as each generation rediscovers their enduring charm.[13]

Hand-decorated WPA items are one-of-a-kind. Because the "workers were given freedom to decorate the mold-made figures in their own fashion, as a result each was in that sense unique."[14] Examination of pieces indicates the difference in each artist's design interpretation.

During the Depression, several artists, who had previously worked in other media, turned to clay which was inexpensive and available. As some of these artists have become well-known, collectors have more eagerly sought their WPA art.

Some art historians, like Paul S. Dornhauser, feel the general quality of work indicates that "no significant artistic innovations grew out of these efforts in the area of pottery."[15] However, the quality of WPA pottery varies widely, depending on the skill and creativity of the individual artist.

Scarcity also affects value. In some states, such as Ohio, WPA ceramics were produced in larger quantity for national distribution to shops and libraries and are, therefore, more plentiful. All North Dakota WPA ceramics are scarce as they were always produced in limited quantities. Many collectors search for artist-signed pieces, which are the most difficult to find.

WPA items are still available because many collectors and dealers are not yet sufficiently aware of them. WPA may be easily passed over at garage sales and flea markets because it blends in with Japanese and other inexpensive ware.

The North Dakota Heritage Center, Bismarck, North Dakota, has become the historical repository for its state WPA. Permanent exhibits in the main gallery display nursery rhymes, signs, and other products. Located on the state capitol grounds, the new structure houses the State Museum, State Archives, and Historical Research Library. (Appendix I)

Ink stamp mark.

Mother Goose 8" nursery rhyme figure; $700.00+. (Courtesy of State Historical Society of North Dakota.)

Old King Cole, 7"; and Fiddlers Three, 5"; $700.00 + each. (Courtesy of State Historical Society of North Dakota.)

Tom Tom the Piper's Son Stole a Pig, 6½"; Peter Peter Pumpkin Eater, 5"; Old Mother Hubbard, 6"; $700.00 each. (Courtesy of State Historical Society of North Dakota.)

Wolf, 9"; and Three Little Pigs, 7"; $700.00 each. (Courtesy of State Historical Society of North Dakota.)

Little Red Riding Hood, 4"; Little Boy Blue, 3½"; $700.00 +. (Courtesy of State Historical Society of North Dakota.)

Little Jack Horner, 4¼"; Mary Had a Little Lamb 5"; Little Miss Muffet, 4"; Jack Be Nimble, 4½"; $700.00+ each. (Courtesy of State Historical Society of North Dakota.)

Sgraffito cobalt blue 9" plate with Native American designs, $800.00+. (Courtesy of State Historical Society of North Dakota.)

Native American motif, black and tan sgraffito 3½" x 7" bowl, $700.00+. (Courtesy of State Historical Society of North Dakota.)

Sgraffito wheat design, 5" vase, $350.00 – 400.00. (Courtesy of State Historical Society of North Dakota.)

Green incised design, 7½" vase, $350.00 – 400.00. (Courtesy of State Historical Society of North Dakota.)

Gloss bright blue 5" vase, $125.00 – 150.00. (Courtesy of State Historical Society of North Dakota.)

Hand-thrown 6" strawberry jar, gloss turquoise, with eight holes, $250.00 – 300.00. (Courtesy of State Historical Society of North Dakota.)

Charcoal hand-thrown 11" vase, signed by Tony Lanz, $250.00 – 300.00. (Courtesy of State Historical Society of North Dakota.)

Green 8" vase with wheat in relief, $300.00 – 350.00. (Courtesy of State Historical Society of North Dakota.)

Gloss creme 7" hand-thrown vase with texture lines and black on handles, $125.00 – 150.00. (Courtesy of State Historical Society of North Dakota.)

Salt and pepper shakers, 2½", $35.00 – 50.00; sugar and creamer, 3", $35.00 – 55.00; two 4" tumblers, $30.00 – 45.00; coffee pot, 7½", $150.00 – 175.00. (Courtesy of State Historical Society of North Dakota.)

2" x 5¼" cereal bowl, $25.00 – 30.00. (Courtesy of State Historical Society of North Dakota.)

4" tumbler, $30.00 – 45.00; 2" custard cup, $20.0 – 25.00; 2" x 5¼" cereal bowl, $25.00 – 30.00.

5½" maroon vase, incised "WPA 1939 ND"; 3" x 7½" tan bowl incised "FJL ND" and ink stamp; 5¾" green vase, signed HD with ink stamp; $85.00 – 100.00 each.

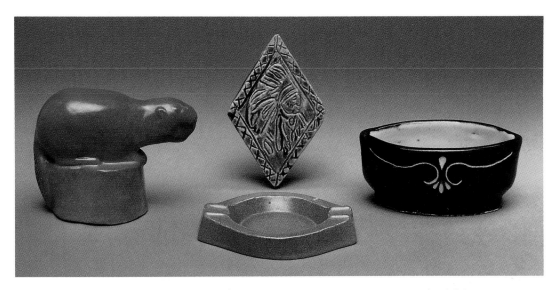

3¼" x 5" beaver, incised "WPA" mark, $250.00 – 300.00; Native American chief 4¼" x 3" paper-weight, marked "BK WPA 1936," $100.00 – 125.00; 4¼" ashtray, "WPA 1938 WD," $35.00 – 50.00; black 2" x 4¾" sgraffito bowl, $100.00 – 150.00.

I saw a potter at his work today
Shaping with rudest hand his whirling clay.
"Ah, gently brother, do not treat me thus;
I, too, was once a man!" I heard it say.

— *Omar Khayyam*

Wahpeton Pottery Company — Rosemeade Pottery

Rosemeade — descriptive tradename for popular North Dakota pottery — instills images of the state flower, the wild prairie rose. Fragrant wild prairie roses, their profuse colorful blossoms growing thickly in the meadows, brightening the unbounded prairies, have become treasured by North Dakotans as their state flower. Laura Taylor, the creator of Rosemeade Pottery, was born in Rosemeade Township, named after the Norwegian hometown of an early settler.

Laura Taylor, who grew up in a rural North Dakota home, became a country one-room school teacher. After her students asked to do art projects, Laura enrolled at Valley City Teachers College to learn drawing — the beginning of a whole new world. Delighted with her first imperfect clay sculpture, a kangaroo, Laura enjoyed going back to teach art to her students.[1]

Laura was inspired to an art career by Glen Lukens, visiting California professor and nationally known studio potter, at a Valley City summer school. After graduating from Valley City, Laura took three years of art and ceramics classes at the University of North Dakota, where she also worked part time as a student assistant.

In 1934, while a student, Laura's donkey clay sculpture was shown at the Ceramic National Exhibition, Syracuse, New York. Further recognition came with her ceramic tile exhibited in the North Dakota building at the Chicago World's Fair.

In 1936, Laura Taylor became state superintendent of the Works Progress Administration Federal Clay Project in Dickinson. Freida Hammers, Laura's former UND instructor, described her WPA work as "naturalistic. She had a natural flair for modeling."[2]

An opportunity to demonstrate pottery making at the 1939 New York World's Fair opened many doors for Laura Taylor. For six months Laura threw pottery on the wheel as part of the WPA display. Laura was also "able to make a valuable study of the modern pottery which the foreign countries displayed in their building on the fair grounds and...continued my study of ceramics in the numerous museums and art galleries of New York City."[3]

Robert J. Hughes, president of the Greater North Dakota Association and a zealous booster of state enterprise, had previously corresponded with Laura Taylor. Since Hughes was interested in pursuing commercial possibilities for native clay, Professor William

Laura Taylor throwing on wheel, New York World's Fair, 1939. Ceramics Department photograph, courtesy of the Elwyn B. Robinson Department of Special Collections, University of North Dakota.

Budge of UND had recommended Laura for her skill and knowledge. Having never met, Hughes watched Laura's World's Fair demonstration. Recognizing an opportunity for local and state development, Hughes proposed a business venture over coffee and donuts at a fairground's food stand and a partnership was formed.

The Wahpeton Pottery Company was founded in January 1940. Robert Hughes, owner of Wahpeton's Globe-Gazette Printing Company and Gift Shop, provided the capital and became president/promoter, business manager. Laura Taylor, a partner and secretary/treasurer, provided the creative genius. The company purchased equipment left after the demise of the Dickinson Clay Products Company when they started their pottery.[4]

At an October 1940 open house, the public was invited to visit the plant. A souvenir horseshoe "WISH US LUCK," surrounding a bowl of prairie roses, with the date on the back, was given to all seven hundred ladies attending.[5]

Clay and romance intermingled with time. In 1942, five young Rosemeade women employees became brides and "this matrimonial contagion spread into the executive offices."[6] This time, Robert Hughes proposed marriage to Laura Taylor and their business relationship expanded to a marital one in 1943.

After being sold first only at the factory, sales of Rosemeade later expanded to the Chahinkapa Park Souvenir Shop in Wahpeton. Rosemeade was later marketed heavily in the upper Midwest, especially in North and South Dakota, Wisconsin, and Minnesota small towns. Marketing eventually expanded to include most states of the Union and many foreign countries, like South Africa. An incentive for *Richland County Farmer-Globe* subscriptions also promoted Rosemeade pottery. "With each full year's subscription paid in advance, your choice of a piece of Rosemeade Pottery FREE!"[7]

The pottery being a success from the beginning, a modern production plant was necessary and built in 1944. With this expansion, Howard Lewis, previously plant superintendent of the Dickinson Clay Products Company, was welcomed as a partner and production manager. Lewis's excellent background as a ceramic engineer and expert technician, along with experience at six previous potteries, led to the formulation of new glazes and development of new products for Rosemeade.

Already in 1953, the *Fargo Forum* newspaper noted that Laura Taylor "has achieved status not only as a North Dakota artist but as a figure of national significance. Critics praise her deft touch and keen eye for capturing the very feel or essence of the subject."[8] Laura described her love for pottery making, "There is something so marvelous in taking a humble little piece of clay and, with a lot of patience, a few simple tools,

and a potter's kiln, making something beautiful and useful."[9]

Laura's honors included a second recognition by the Ceramic National Exhibition of Syracuse, New York, with two hand-thrown fish in 1951. Laura Taylor Hughes received the 1951 Citation Award of the American Artists Professional League. Being featured in a full-page color photo in the September 1951 article "North Dakota Comes into its Own" in the *National Geographic Magazine* was a further honor.

"A farm girl who at an early age fell in love with the native flowers, birds, animals, and scenes of North Dakota,"[10] Laura's inspirations were many. Laura worked from real life whenever possible, as well as sketches, pictures, and mounted animals and birds. On her world-wide travels, Laura was constantly collecting ideas and reference materials. On annual trips across the United States, Laura chatted with dealers, getting their ideas for new designs.

Promoting good labor-management relationships and stimulating creativity, Laura also encouraged employee participation. Workers often gave ideas for new designs or new details for old designs.

Loyal employees took pride in their work. A newspaper notes, "When a new item is being produced, the factory teems with excitement and the employees are the first ones to buy the new pieces."[11] All employees understood the complete pottery-making operation as they were trained in all phases. Their jobs were rotated on a monthly basis, diminishing assembly-line boredom. Employee turnover was extremely low, with a waiting list of job applicants.

Although Robert Hughes was also a potter, he did not do Rosemeade design work. Laura did the vast majority of the designing, but at least one other artist also produced designs. Vera Gethman, from Gorham, North Dakota, a talented sculptress of western scenes, worked for the pottery temporarily. Gethman's love for horses, which she studied during her life on the range, shines through in her equine designs. Laura Taylor described Gethman's skills, "she gives animation to clay in her hands and distills the nostrils of the animal with the rarefied air of the plateau regions of the state."[12]

Glazes varied from soft mattes to lustrous glosses, with glaze names like meadow green, dusty rose, and mirror blue. A Rosemeade advertising brochure described Harvest Gold as "a blending of amber and red which when fired at different temperatures, produces effects as varied and unexpected as a ripening field of grain or autumn leaves after frost." A dark metallic bronze glaze with gold highlights was brought from Broadmoor Pottery, according to Howard Lewis. However, the vivid colorful hues are the most distinctive.

These unique colorful gloss glazes set Rosemeade pottery apart, making it easily recognizable. Metal oxides painted under the glazes "became partially absorbed in the glaze and run slightly in firing, creating a true ceramic effect."[13] Marion Nelson further described the buff-colored clay body as showing "through enough to bring the applied colors into harmony. The whites are painted with slips, which stand out as bright accents on the blended grounds."

During the early years, Laura experimented with glazes, applying her University of North Dakota knowledge. After Howard Lewis joined the company, he took over glaze experimentation and production. Because Lewis concocted glazes to fit the specific clay properties, instead of using commercial glazes, most shrinkage and crazing were eliminated.

Most Rosemeade was cast in plaster molds made from Laura's original clay models. Some cast pieces were deliberately made to look handmade. According to a local newspaper, Laura Taylor would shape the prototype bowl or vase on the potter's wheel. Then a mold was cast of the slightly irregular model "to retain much of the quaint irregularity of hand thrown work."[14]

Laura made a few hand-thrown Rosemeade pieces, especially in the early days. Swirl pieces were also made on the wheel.

North Dakota is reflected in many of Laura's designs. The state bird, meadowlark, appears on various Rosemeade items from plaques to pins. The flicker-tail, a tiny, agile rodent also known as the ground squirrel and named the state animal, is another Rosemeade motif. Souvenirs of the state capital, a slender skyscraper shaft jutting starkly from the prairies in Bismarck, celebrate its unusual architecture. Peace Garden salt and peppers, souvenirs, and ashtrays recognize the International Peace Garden near Bottineau, a landscaped park which symbolizes lasting friendship between the United States and Canada. Rosemeade produced buffalo in many sizes, using both sand and white clay and three glazes — gloss, matte, and bronze.

Theodore Roosevelt National Park, the only national park in North Dakota and its foremost tourist attraction, inspired several Rosemeade commemoratives. American Guild writers described the Park Badlands as "one of the most extraordinary topographies on the surface of the earth."[15] As a young man, Theodore Roosevelt spent time in North Dakota hunting and ranching. His former home, the Roosevelt Cabin, including much Rooseveltiana, resides on the state capital grounds. Rosemeade items included a log cabin facsimile incense burner, National Park mug, and Theodore Roosevelt plate, paperweight, and mug.

A Rosemeade teddy bear figurine appears alone and on ashtrays. The teddy bear was named for Theodore Roosevelt, who hunted and enjoyed observing bears in the wild. A famous political cartoon by Clifford Berryman portrayed Roosevelt and a bear cub, sparking an idea for a stuffed animal—"Teddy's bear."[16]

Pheasants became synonymous with Rosemeade for many. Laura described the Chinese ring-necked salt and pepper shakers as "undoubtedly our best seller."[17] A salesman first suggested the game bird design in 1942, with sales expected mainly in South Dakota. However, a local newspaper soon noted that "souvenir birds are proving almost as popular with sportsmen visiting here for the pheasant hunting as the real article" as hunters in both North and South Dakota sought the souvenir natural plumage pheasants.[18] Although the small cock and hen pheasant salt and pepper sets were the most popular, the pheasant was also sold in such variations as plaques, figures, and vases. By 1953, more than 500,000 Rosemeade pheasants in 19 different designs had been sold to an eager public.[19]

As the pheasants had started their popularity with hunters, so Taylor's fish were popular with fishermen, especially sportsmen visiting the Minnesota resort areas. Attention to detail was such that a local newspaper noted the small differences in jaw and notches between fins which distinguish Taylor's rendition of the large mouth bass in comparison with her small mouth bass.[20]

By identifying special niches of interest and creating items for specific regions, organizations, and places, the company produced several successes. Examples illustrate how national in scope production became. Turkeys were made for the National Turkey Federation; pandas for Chicago's Brookfield Zoo; Rocky Mountain goats and bears for Glacier National Park; and tulips for Holland, Michigan. Several items illustrated state themes, like alligators and sailfish for Florida; poppies for California; sunflowers for Kansas; quail for Georgia; pelicans for Louisiana and Texas; and mallards for Minnesota. Although made for special sales, most found "generally large sales throughout the country."[21]

Rosemeade has become well known for its quality salt and pepper shakers. Mike Schneider, in *The Complete Salt and Pepper Shaker Book*, stated that Rosemeade "created and marketed some of the finest figural shakers that have ever been made."[22] Animals, especially wild species, were abundant, perhaps as a result of Laura's rural background. The wide variety of realistic animals includes wolves, mountain goats, fawns, elephants, raccoons, zebras, rabbits, and cats.

Laura Taylor's songbird salt and pepper shakers include bluebirds, goldfinches, and chickadees, with robins the most popular. Laura created several regional bird favorites, like the flamingos for Florida.

According to Schneider, "Rosemeade led the fleet in attempting to net the fish buyers...You would have to go a long way to beat the quality of Rosemeade's fish shakers, both naturalistic and stylized version."[23]

Her fish include walleye, trout, muskies, Northern pike, croppies, bluegills, and muskellunges.

Although mythical lumberjack Paul Bunyan and Native American heads appear to be Laura's only shakers featuring people, Rosemeade's salt and pepper shakers covered many other themes. Vegetables include peppers, cucumbers, potatoes, brussel sprouts, and corn. The prairie rose, cactus, and tulip became designs for flower shakers. Other shakers show windmills, and sailboats.

In 1950, Laura Taylor started decorating molded ashtrays with dog heads she had copied from the National Geographic Magazine. She went on to design 12 different sets of dog head salt and pepper shakers including greyhound, chow chow, Mexican chihuahua, dalmatian, Scottish terrier, pekinese, English bulldog, bloodhound, English toy terrier, wire haired terrier, Boston terrier, and English setter. A photo in the September 1951 National Geographic shows Laura working on these shakers,[24] after having been sent home to put on a more photogenically colorful smock. According to North Dakota Horizons, the line was expected to be a big seller but was not.[25]

At peak production, 27 employees were producing 1,400 pieces daily. From 200 – 250 different designs and a wide variety of products were created. Figurines, some from shaker forms and others being available only as figurines, head a long list of Rosemeade products. Everything from lamps, planters, wall pockets, jewelry, creamers and sugar bowls, bookends, pitchers, candlesticks, spoonrests, banks, bells, and snack sets to cotton dispensers demonstrate the wide diversity.

The company name was changed from Wahpeton Pottery Company to Rosemeade Potteries in 1953. According to Robert Hughes, it was "too confusing for our distant patrons and salesmen to remember two names so we decided to concentrate on the name of our product."[26] With its connection to the state flower and a county township, this tradename also provided good company name recognition for state residents.

As was true of many potteries of the time, the company produced quan-

Joe McLaughlin. Courtesy of Joe McLaughlin.

tities of advertising items, especially ashtrays. National parks, states, banks, golf courses, centennials, feed, chicken, oil, and ice cream companies placed special orders.

Many of the Rosemeade items became popular as Christmas gifts. The Hughes themselves used the fawn motif, popular in both figurines and salt and pepper shakers, on their personal Christmas card sent in the 1950s.

Howard Lewis designed and created hand-thrown swirl clay vases and pitchers, similar in technique to those of Niloak Pottery, where he had been employed and those he created as the Badlands line at Dickinson Clay Products Company. According to Lewis, these swirl pieces were only made for a short time in limited quantity.

When Howard Lewis left the company in 1956, Joe McLaughlin, who had previously worked for Red Wing Potteries as assistant ceramic engineer and company foreman, was hired as production manager. McLaughlin, ceramic engineering graduate of Ohio State University with experience as plant manager at Hyalyn Porcelain, Hickory, North Carolina, brought new concepts to Rosemeade.

After admiring wildlife designs in the newspaper by Les Kouba, one of Minnesota's most famous wildlife artists, Joe McLaughlin visited him and asked about the possibility of making Rosemeade decals from his designs. Kouba declined a fee, replying "I'd be proud to do it."[27] Thus, Les L. Kouba designed and signed three pheasant, duck, and fish decals used on Rosemeade pottery.

Kouba decals were used on various products. Joe McLaughlin stated that glazed white tiles were purchased. Decals were applied at Rosemeade and the pieces fired. These tiles were sold as both trivets and wall plaques. The tiles were also mounted in purchased walnut and birch frames and sold to the public. Other items made at Rosemeade from North Dakota clay, like mugs, were also decorated with Kouba decals.[28]

In 1958, white clay from Kentucky was shipped to Rosemeade. McLaughlin found molding pottery with North Dakota clay difficult. Molds could only be used once a day as adding the large quantities of necessary water to the clay slowed drying. With the white clay, the molds could be used two to three times a day. This clay also shrunk less than the North Dakota clay and produced a whiter final product.

Under Joe McLaughlin's direction, the company also started using other decals as decoration. The white Kentucky clay was more suitable for decals. The decals made for Rosemeade by a Fort Smith, Arkansas, company were used the last three years of Rosemeade's production. Examples include Dakota Territory Centennial 1861 – 1961 memorabilia, including plates, ashtrays, and trivets, all made at Rosemeade Potteries from white clay and decorated with the Centennial logo decals.

The majority of Rosemeade pottery was still made from North Dakota yellow sand clay from a huge deposit near Mandan. But white clay was used mainly on specialty advertising items, until the company closed, according to McLaughlin.[29]

Joe McLaughlin reminisced, "The pottery industry itself was fascinating because things never seemed set. Firing conditions would change. Clay mixtures needed adjusting and glazes needed to be developed. It was very satisfying to start something new and see it become beautiful and salable."[30]

After Laura Taylor Hughes died of cancer in 1959, production continued until 1961. Joe McLaughlin did the designing of mainly specialty items with nine employees.

Already in 1953, "Copies of Rosemeade pieces, many of them quite crude, pop up now and then on gift ware counters."[31] Joe McLaughlin stated that by 1956, "Sales and demand for Rosemeade had declined due to cheap Japanese imports. For example, we found items for sale in stores that were copies of our wares. They were evidently made in molds from our pieces because they were smaller due to firing shrinkage. They were being retailed at prices less than our whole-sale pieces."[32] A new state minimum wage law and Laura's death also contributed to the company closing. The salesroom was open until 1964 as Betty McLaughlin became the last Rosemeade employee, helping Robert Hughes close out the pottery.[33] The Richland County Historical Museum continued to sell remaining stock in the 90s.

Both Howard Lewis and Joe McLaughlin taught at the North Dakota State College of Science, Wahpeton, after leaving Rosemeade. Howard Lewis taught for 12 years and died in 1993. Joe McLaughlin taught in the architectural department for 20 years before retiring and moving to Arizona.

The Richland County Historical Museum became the Hughes legacy. Already in 1946, Robert and Laura Hughes met with local residents to discuss forming a county historical society to keep alive the early history of pioneers. Laura Hughes kept the dream of a museum alive, and during her long illness, made plans to will money for its building. After Laura's death, Robert Hughes became a major benefactor of the museum which opened on July 1, 1965. The museum displays a major Rosemeade collection. (Appendix I)

Rosemeade pottery, a successful sales enterprise in its own time, continues to be a popular collectible. As the company listened to its employees and the public, expanding and introducing product lines, Rosemeade appealed to the public then and collectors now.

Much Rosemeade is marked with an ink stamp of the company name in black or blue lettering on the bottom. Several variations, including the words "North Dakota," also appear. Paper stickers, showing the prairie rose and "Rosemeade NO. DAK." were used frequently. However, since these stickers were often lost or removed, many Rosemeade pieces are unmarked. A few pieces were signed or initialed by the artist.

Unmarked pieces can usually be recognized by the beach-sand color of the clay on the unglazed bottoms, as well as their overall design features and glaze colors. In recent years, people have brought items they considered to be Rosemeade to the Richland County Historical Museum, where paper stickers have been applied. Questions have arisen regarding the identity of some items with paper Rosemeade stickers. The collector should again rely on clay color, shape, and glaze.

At first, imperfect pieces were thrown into a wheelbarrow and destroyed after quality inspection by Laura. However, "many pieces were salvaged by employees so a decision was made to sell the 'imperfects' or 'seconds.'"[34] Newspaper ads of the time advertised "seconds," which could be purchased only in Wahpeton. "As always, no imperfect pieces of Rosemeade Pottery or seconds are sold to dealers. All such pieces have always been sold at the factory salesroom."[35]

Products particularly collectible include Rosemeade salt and pepper shakers. Swirl Rosemeade was limited in quantity. The small ceramic pins are also difficult to find. Small Rosemeade items are attractive to some collectors because their size makes storage and display easier.

Laura Taylor Hughes chose subjects which continually fascinate people — animals, birds, fish — and modeled original authentic reproductions of their living counterparts. These innovative designs were then accurately hand painted in nature's vivid coloring. Perhaps this is the secret of Rosemeade's success as people in the 40s, 50s, and today have identified with these meaningful images of their world.

Wahpeton Pottery Company – Rosemeade Pottery Marks

Dealer's 6½" sign, $1,000.00+; pink fish, salt and pepper shakers, 2¾", $50.00 – 65.00; pin cushion cactus, shakers, 1", $35.00 – $45.00; pink tulips, shakers, 2¼", $40.00 – 50.00; green dolphin, shakers, 2½", $50.00 – $65.00.

Bird salt and pepper shakers. Large 3¼" chickens; 3¾" flamingos; 2½" white chickens; 2" swans; 2½" chickens; 2½" quail; 3½" ducks. $65.00 – 85.00 each.

Art Deco wolfhound 6½" x 7½" bookends, $350.00 – 500.00 pair.

Mallard plaques, duck 5" x 5½" and drake 6½" x 7½", $800.00+.

Early glaze. 3½" pitcher and 4" vase with aqua interior, $50.00 – 75.00 each.

Figurines. Solid 4" pony, $125.00 – 150.00; 3" bear bank, $450.00 – 500.00; small Rocky Mountain goat on base, 2¾" x 2¾", $150.00 – 175.00; solid 2¾" dog, $75.00 – 100.00; two cats, 2" x 2", $20.00 – 25.00 set; 1¼" elephant, $60.00 – 75.00; two skunks 1½" and ¾", $20.00 – 25.00 set; two penguins 1" and ¾", $30.00 – 40.00 set.

Planters. 8" deer, $50.00 – 75.00; 7½" peacock, $150.00 – 200.00; 4¾" x 4¾" swan, $50.00 – 75.00; 4½" x 6" dove, $125.00 – 150.00; 4" x 5¼" log with deer, $50.00 – 60.00.

Large vases. 9½" green textured, $80.00 – 100.00; 8½" pink and gray, $75.00 – 85.00; 9" bronze vase, $60.00 – 75.00.

Chinese ring-necked pheasants. Large 7" x 11½" cock, $250.00 – 300.00; two 3¾", $25.00 – 35.00 each; 2¾" salt and pepper shakers, $25.00 – 35.00.

Hen pheasant 3½" x 11½", $200.00 – 250.00.

Spoon rests. 3¾" pansy; 5½" tulip; 3¼" x 5½" flying pheasant; 2½" ladyslipper; 4" wild rose. $50.00 – 75.00 each.

Hand-painted 4" zebra on bisque made in limited quantity, according to Howard Lewis, $350.00 – 375.00.

Swirl. Two-color 4" vase with top and bottom rims; 3¼" pitcher; two-color 3" vase; 2¾" pitcher; 3¾" vase. $125.00 – 150.00 each.

Mark on swirl pieces.

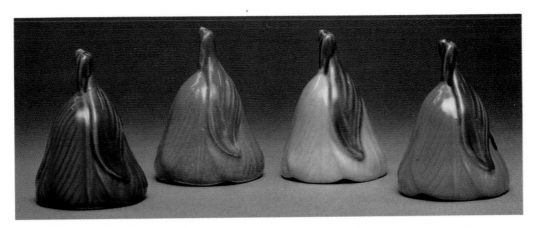

Art Nouveau 3¾" tulip tea bells. Maroon, blue, yellow, pink, $125.00 – 150.00 each.

Animal salt and pepper shakers, 2" to 3½". Cats, leaping deer, oxen, rabbits, lying deer, ponies, mice, $55.00 – 75.00 each.

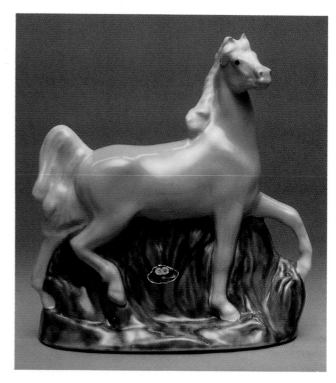

Palomino horse 9½" figurine with cut-out foliage, $450.00 – 500.00.

Palomino 9½" television lamp, $475.00 – 525.00.

Pins. Mallard duck, 3½" x 3½"; mallard head, 2" x 2"; bear, 2" x 2"; meadowlark, 2" x 2"; prairie rose, 2" x 2". $375.00 – 450.00 each. (Courtesy of State Historical Society of North Dakota.)

7" wheat vase, $60.00 – 75.00; 2½" corn sugar and creamer, $35.00 – 55.00; 6¾" x 5¼" wheat dish, $75.00 – 85.00; 1½" cucumber salt and pepper shakers, $50.00 – 60.00; 1½" brussel sprouts salt and pepper shakers, $40.00 – 50.00.

Minnesota Centennial memorabilia. Brown 3" mug, $40.00 – 65.00; light green 3" mug, $40 – 65.00; 3" pink mug, $40.00 – 65.00; pink 7" jug, $80.00 – 100.00; 8" dark green spoon rest, $40.00 – 65.00. The pieces display Minnesota symbols, like the state logo, Norway pine, and ladyslipper.

2" to 3½" dog head salt and pepper shakers. Wire haired fox terrier, English setter, Scottish terrier, chow chow, greyhound, $40.00 – 85.00 pair.

2" to 3½" dog head salt and pepper shakers. English bull dog, pekinese, English toy spaniel, $40.00 – 85.00 pair.

Dog head mark.

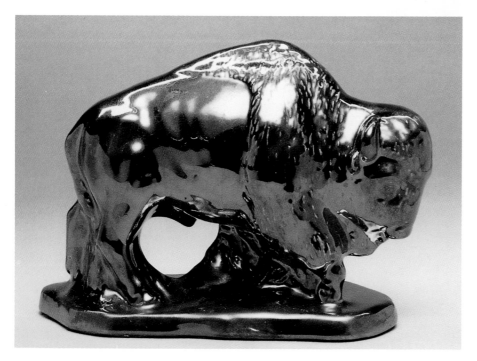

Bronze 6½" x 8½" buffalo, $400.00 – 500.00.

Wall pockets. 5" deer, $50.00 – 75.00; 4¼" 4-H Club, $75.00 – 100.00; leaves, $50.00 – 75.00.

Figurines. 2¾" x 4" skunk, $20.00 – 30.00; 4½" x 6½" fighting cock, $50.00 – 75.00; 2½" x 3" solid elephant, $75.00 – 95.00; prairie dogs, 1½" and 1¼", $50.00 – 60.00 set; seals, 1½", 1¼", and ½", $40.00 – 50.00 set; bears, 1" and 1¾", $40.00 – 50.00 set; mice, 1" and 1½", $20.00 – 30.00 set.

2½" quail with feather top knot salt and pepper shakers, $75.00 – 100.00.

Ewald Dairy 6" pitcher made in various sizes to advertise Minneapolis dairy, $100.00 – 150.00.

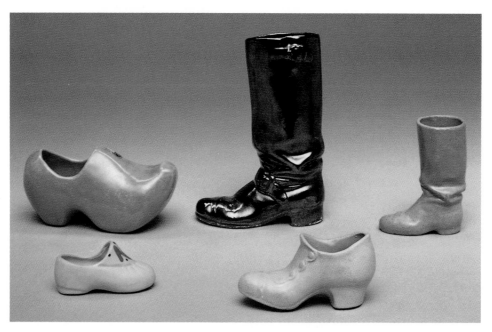

Wooden-like 2" x 5½" shoe, $40.00 – 50.00; bronze 6½" Ranger's boot, $65.00 – 75.00; brown 3¾" Ranger's boot, $30.00 – 40.00; decorated 1¼" x 3¼" shoe, $20.00 – 30.00; blue button slipper, 1¾" x 4¼", $40.00 – 50.00.

Turkeys. 3¾" cream pitcher and 4½" sugar bowl, $135.00 – 150.00; covered 4½" cranberry dish with spoon notch, $125.00 – 150.00; 3" salt and pepper shakers, $50.00 – 75.00.

2¼" Paul Bunyan and Babe the Blue Ox salt and pepper shakers, $75.00 – 85.00.

Fish wall plaques, 3½" x 6", $150.00 – 250.00 each.

4" salt and pepper shakers, $30.00 – 40.00; 2" sugar and creamer, $25.00 – 35.00; 2" salt and pepper shakers, advertised as "Modern Design," $25.00 – 35.00; fish hors d'oeuvre holder, 2¼" x 3¾", $50.00 – 75.00.

Vases made to look hand thrown. 6" pinkish peach, $40.00 – 60.00; 4" ruffled rim, $35.00 – 55.00.

Bronze 7¼" doe, $50.00 – 75.00; 5" rabbit cotton dispenser, $100.00 – 125.00; 8" white clay "Indian 'God of Peace' Saint Paul Minnesota," replica of 44-foot-tall St. Paul City Hall and Courthouse statue, recently renamed Vision of Peace, $125.00 – 150.00.

White 5" rabbit cotton dispenser with pink hand-painted ear interiors and eyes, $125.00 – 150.00.

Tan mug, 4", $30.00 – 40.00; 2" rose mini pitcher, $25.00 – 35.00; pink 3¾" pitcher with braided handle, $40.00 – 60.00; blue pinched handle 2¼" pitcher, $30.00 – 40.00; 5¼" tan pitcher, $30.00 – 40.00.

Egyptian design 5½" wall vase advertised as "a youth serenades with a song" and color described as antique gray, lined with porous bisque planter, $150.00 – 200.00.

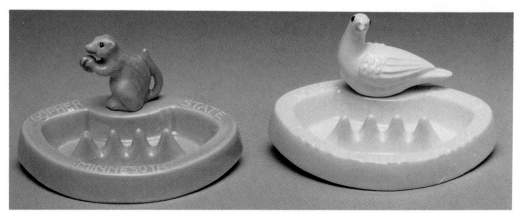

5" ashtrays with attached figures. Gopher on "GOPHER STATE MINNESOTA," dove on "North Dakota Peace Garden State," $150.00 – 200.00 each.

Ashtrays. Minnesota Centennial, 3¾" x 4¼", $35.00 – 55.00; Rosemeade Pottery's own 5" advertising ashtray, $45.00 – 65.00; blue 4¼" wheat, $35.00 – 45.00.

3¾" vase with molded decoration, $50.00 – 75.00; pink 4" x 4½" flower arranger, $25.00 – 35.00; 4¼" x 5" pink basket, $40.00 – 55.00; blue 3½" vase, $30.00 – 40.00; green 4¾" x 3¾" pansy ring, $20.00 – 30.00; 1¾" x 4¾" purple nut cup, $20.00 – 30.00.

Blue 3" vase with holes for flowers, $25.00 – 35.00; bronze 3" vase, $25.00 – 35.00; 4" rose watering can with rabbit molded design, $50.00 – 75.00; blue 4½" bud vase, $20.00 – 30.00; pink 7½" bud vase, $25.00 – 35.00; 3½" x 7½" planter with bird flower frog, $50.00 – 75.00.

Pieces made by Laura Taylor at UND. 5¼" round plates, $150.00-200.00 each, with buffalo, sheaf of oats, and Native American chief; hand-molded 8" rooster, marked "LAT 127," $750.00+.

Les Kouba decal 6" pheasant tiles in 8" and 10" wooden frames, $80.00 – 100.00 each.

Wooden framed mallard 6" tile, $80.00 – 100.00.

Kouba 6" pheasant and mallard wallhangings, $50.00 – 75.00 each.

Dakota Territory Centennial 7" ashtray, $65.00 – 75.00.

Rosemeade Pottery Booklet

ROSEMEADE OFFERS ITS CUSTOMERS

A WIDE SELECTION·

Hand-Thrown Glazed Ware

VASES, *assorted shapes*	$ .50 to 1.00
BUD VASES	.50
CANDLE HOLDERS, *per pair*	1.00
BOWLS	.50 to 2.50
FLOWER BASKETS	.50 to 1.00
PITCHERS	.50 to 1.50
CREAM AND SUGAR SETS	1.00
HATS	.75

Hand-Thrown Bad Lands Ware

VASES AND BOWLS	.50 to 1.50
PITCHERS	.50
CREAM AND SUGAR SETS	1.00
ASH TRAYS	.50 to .75
HATS	.50

Ceramic Figures and Novelty Items

FIGURES, ANIMALS, BIRDS, ETC.	.35 to 10.00
FIGURE AND VASE COMBINATION	1.00 to 2.50
PLAQUES	.75 to 1.25
WALL POCKETS	.50 to 1.50
BOOK-ENDS, *per pair*	3.00 to 4.00
ASH TRAYS	.35 to .75
SALTS AND PEPPERS, *plain and novelty shapes*	.75 to 1.00

> **THE WAHPETON POTTERY COMPANY**
> Was organized in January, 1940 with MR. R. J. HUGHES, a native North Dakotan, as its president. The enthusiastic reception accorded its wares has given the industry a healthy, steady growth. * * * * * * * *

Rosemeade
POTTERY

I saw a potter at his work today
Shaping with rudest hand his whirling clay.
"Ah, gently brother, do not treat me thus;
I, too, was once a man!" I heard it say.

—OMAR KHAYYAM

ROSEMEADE POTTERY is as native to North Dakota as her state flower—the wild rose—which furnished the inspiration for its name. The fine quality of pottery clay from which it is made comes from near Mandan, North Dakota. Many of the designs were inspired by the state's rose covered meadows, her rolling wheat fields and her scenic Bad Lands. Even the designers of Rosemeade are native North Dakotans .... LAURA TAYLOR, manager of the Wahpeton Pottery, creates the original models for the modern ceramic figures as well as the designs for the general line of pottery. VERA GETHMAN of Gorham, North Dakota, uses animals from Wahpeton's Chahinkapa Park as living models for her small naturalistic animal figures; wild horses, which roam at large near her ranch home in the Bad Lands, for her spirited horses .... Much of the Rosemeade ware is fashioned on the potter's wheel. This ancient method, known as "throwing", gives each hand-made piece a charm and individuality of its own .... Glazes used on the pottery are the result of much experimentation at the Wahpeton factory. Their subdued hues give a suitable finish to the excellent design and fine workmanship which characterize each piece of Rosemeade.

Rosemeade Pottery Booklet

ROSEMADEE GIFTWARE
A WIDE SELECTION

AMERICAN WILDLIFE NUMBERS—
This group is made up of native birds and animals in the form of salt and pepper sets, wall plaques, ceramic figures and jewelry. The Chinese ring necked pheasant and mallards, with their gay plumage, are particularly lifelike in design and coloring.

FOR FLOWER ARRANGEMENTS—
Rosemeade florists items are decorative as well as useful. There are vases, jardinieres and wall vases in historic Egyptian design with modern styling. Also bowls and candle holders with matching flower holders in bird, fish and animal designs.

CREAM AND SUGAR SETS—
Attractive designs and gay colors characterize these sets. With some of the cream and sugar sets there are matching salts and peppers, ash trays or tea bells.

TEA BELLS—
A tulip bloom with its simple bell shaped form was the inspiration for one of these bells. Others are in the shape of animals or birds. All have musical tones.

BOOKENDS—
The well designed bookends are beautifully glazed in black, brown, wine and bronze. They are weighted and are finished with felt bases. Sturdy and practical, they will really hold books.

The articles mentioned above are only part of the line of beautiful Rosemeade Giftware. There are souvenirs for tourists, items for collectors and gifts for every occasion.

THE WAHPETON POTTERY COMPANY
Wahpeton, North Dakota

Rosemeade
POTTERY

I saw a potter at his work today
Shaping with rudest hand his whirling clay.
"Ah, gently brother, do not treat me thus;
I, too, was once a man!" I heard it say.

—OMAR KHAYYAM

A WORD ABOUT ROSEMEADE GIFTWARE - - -

ROSEMEADE POTTERY is as native to North Dakota as her state flower—The Wild Rose—which furnished the inspiration for its name. A light burning pottery clay of a fine quality from the abundant clay beds of Western North Dakota is used in its manufacture. The pottery designs are the original creations of Laura Taylor Hughes, a native North Dakotan. The state's flower strewn meadows, her scenic Bad Lands, western ranch life and wild game and song birds have inspired many of the pottery designs.

Each piece is first modeled in clay with careful attention given to the outstanding characteristics of the figure which is being made, or to the purpose for which the article is to be used. From the clay models hollow plaster moulds are made. The ware is formed in these moulds by the method known as slip-casting. The clay is prepared by soaking it in water and straining it through a fine sieve. This liquid clay is called slip. The dry mould is filled with slip and it is allowed to stand until a layer of clay has adhered to the inside of the mould. The rest of the slip is poured out and the layer of clay which remains inside becomes the piece of pottery. After the cast piece has been removed from the mould the rough edges are taken off, any imperfections are corrected and the piece is thoroughly dried. It is then given its first or bisque firing. The firing is at a red hot temperature that fuses and hardens the clay and it is then ready for the glazing.

The glaze is a mixture of minerals compounded in such a way that they will melt together when brought to high temperatures. The glaze is applied by dipping, spraying or brushing and the ware is then returned to the kiln for the second firing, this time at temperatures even higher than the first. The utmost care is given to each phase of the whole process. Some of the Rosemeade Giftware is finished in softly shaded matt glazes, other pieces in dark bronze or lustrous gloss glazes in colorful hues. The finished product is an article of beauty, of attractive design and fine workmanship; an American product which its manufacturers are proud to offer to admirers of beautiful things.

The Wahpeton Pottery Company, manufacturers of Rosemeade pottery, was organized in 1940 and began business in Wahpeton, North Dakota that year. Its officers are R. J. Hughes, president; Laura Taylor Hughes, treasurer and vice president; and Howard S. Lewis, secretary and production manager.

Turn, turn, my wheel! All things must change
To something new, to something strange;
Nothing that is can pause or stay!
The moon will wax, the moon will wane,
The mist and cloud will turn to rain,
The rain to mist and cloud again,
Tomorrow be today.

— H. W. Longfellow
Keramos

Ceramics By Messer

An old farm chicken coop became the unlikely home for quality North Dakota pottery — Ceramics by Messer. A native North Dakotan, born in Buffalo Springs, Joe Messer moved to Bowman as a toddler. After serving three years in the navy, Joe took his Bowman bride, Eunice Olson, to Kansas City, where he studied at the Kansas City Art Institute. Majoring in oil painting and studying ceramics and sculpture, Joe graduated with honors in 1951. Eunice learned art techniques through her job at Hallmark. Returning to Bowman, Joe and Eunice sold their furniture and car to finance their ceramics enterprise and moved in with Eunice's supportive parents, the Olsons. When Harry Olson told his son-in-law, "Half the chicken coop is yours—if you can make it do," Messer decided "the smelly old chicken coop could well make first substance of his dream."[1]

Working together from the start, the husband-wife team learned new carpentry skills as they converted the old coop into a studio. Because they couldn't afford equipment, the Messers, "starting on the proverbial shoestring, used ingenuity, resourcefulness, and hard work."[2] Messer built a chimney and two kilns, shaping and fitting each fire brick by hand and then rebuilding and adjusting several times. Using an old Ford transmission and brake drum, Messer designed and constructed a potter's wheel. A Maytag washer mixed the casting clay, while the washer wringers ground the glazes. Discarded files and screw drivers became turning and trimming tools.

According to Eunice Messer, full production began in fall 1952.[3] Joe did the designing, wheel-throwing, mold-making, and some painting. All casting and trimming of molded pieces and some hand painting were Eunice's responsibility. Eunice's mother, Leota, also helped with the trimming. Kiln opening became a family event, with Eunice's father also coming home to await the surprises.

Already that first autumn, the pottery was an instant success. After their wares were marketed in a few local

Joe Messer at the wheel. Courtesy of Eunice Messer.

The Messer chicken coop studio. Courtesy of Eunice Messer.

stores, the many orders were hard to fill. They hired four salesmen on commission. Major marketing states were North Dakota, South Dakota, Wyoming, Montana, and California, as well as Canada. The salesmen would come to Bowman once a month to leave orders and get merchandise.

Additional working space was needed by early summer of 1953. The chickens on the other side of the coop had sometimes tried to return to old roosting places in the studio side with disastrous results. Now, these chickens were displaced to a new location and the studio expanded to use the entire coop.

In the summer of 1954, the pottery moved into a former double gas station and mechanic's garage on Highway 12, the major road to the Black Hills. The gift shop was housed on one side of the garage and the studio on the other. When the large garage door to the studio was open, tourists would stop at "The Pot Shop" and watch Joe at the potter's wheel. People would order pieces and then pick up the fired items on their way home. They had all the orders they could handle from sales at their own shop and local stores to both tourists and "a very supportive Bowman community."[4] Signs on the highway directed tourists to their shop.

Joe and Eunice purchased a lightweight potter's wheel and demonstrated pottery making throughout their community. Having attended country schools himself, Joe particularly enjoyed the response of country school children. Their demonstrations were also popular with such groups as the American Association of University Women, homemakers, and 4-H clubs.

Joe and Eunice made an outstanding team, working together toward a common goal. Both had artistic talent. Joe had received the art training and Eunice "absorbed everything I could from him." Every night, even after a late kiln firing, they would sit and relax with a cup of tea, talking over the day. "We would get so excited thinking of what we were going to make and do, we could hardly sleep."[5]

Eunice found her own ways to help finance the pottery operation. For example, while they were remodeling the gas station/garage, she made and sold enamel jewelry. By growing house plants in their pottery flower pots, Eunice made them more salable.

White clay mixtures from Pennsylvania were fired at 2500° F to produce gleaming porcelain-finished pottery. According to Eunice, Joe formulated the mixtures himself, sometimes from ten ingredients. After Joe originally designed figures in clay, several plaster molds were made of each sculpture. Messer also experimented with native white clay to produce his distinctive high-quality natural glazes.

Joe Messer created naturalistic replicas of animals typical of the area, sculpting from life whenever possible. His Hereford, Holstein, and Black Angus cattle were modeled after actual local farm animals. For example, Harry Olson staked his Hereford bull outside the studio window for Joe to sketch and model. Ranchers ordered custom-made cattle figurines with their own brands carved into the correct position.

Devil's Tower salt and pepper shakers are other examples of Joe Messer's working from nature to create realism. Eunice tells about Joe traveling to the monument, where he spent three days at the base, perfecting his model. Wyoming's Devil's Tower, an 865 feet high volcanic rock arising from the prairie, was this nation's first national monument, set aside for the American people in 1906 by President Theodore Roosevelt.

Wildlife depiction reflected Messer's hobby of hunting and trapping — rabbits, prairie dogs, turtles, buck and doe antelope, coyotes, and ducks — even the fanciful creature of many hunter's imagination — the jackelope, sold only in Wyoming.

Several of the animal figures were made into salt and pepper shakers. Salt and pepper shakers had been the first thing Joe made — gray and white ghosts with shaker holes in their eyes for Halloween sales. Chef, Devil's Tower, and oil derrick salt and peppers were also made. Salt and pepper grain elevators advertised North Dakota towns like Killdeer, Hettinger, and Rhame. New English and Miles City were advertised on miniature gas pump figurines. Some salt and peppers were used as promotional giveaways to merchants' best customers. An unusual 1953 wall plaque with hooks for keys was sold only in Dickinson to promote that city. A man tips his cowboy hat — "Howdy! I'm Dick from Dickinson."

Native white clay, dug by Joe and Eunice near

Eunice and Joe working as a team on a porcelain figurine. Courtesy of Eunice Messer.

Bowman was used on hand-thrown stoneware — vases, sugar and creamers, teapots, mugs, bottles, jars with lids, pitchers, bowls, cups and saucers, and planters. The native clay was so pure, only water had to be added. Some vases were so large, they had to be made in two parts. Other vases were so tiny they were made with only two fingers. Since no two wheel-thrown pieces are the same, a tag was attached to each, indicating "one-of-a-kind" original.

Marks include an impressed black ink "MESSER BOWMAN, N. DAK.," impressed "MESSER©" with date and hand-incised "MESSER." Silver stickers of "CERAMICS BY MESSER" were sometimes used. Pieces were occasionally dated.

Production, which grew to approximately 50 different items, ceased in 1956 because of low-fired Japanese imports competing for the market. Their molds were sold to one buyer, their inventory depleted, and the Messers left Bowman.

For 30 years, Joe was a commercial designer for the Jostens company. Living in various locations, Joe taught community art classes and continued his art work in sculpture, oils, and watercolors, painting portraits, landscapes and still lifes. The family worked together in artistic endeavors until Joe died in 1987.

The Pioneer Trails Regional Museum in Bowman, North Dakota, recently developed an exhibit of Messer pottery. Examples are displayed and more sought. (Appendix I)

Several of Joe Messer's early creations were included in the November 1951, Bismarck American Art Week Show. The exhibitors' list reads like a who's who of this era's North Dakota potters — Laura Taylor Hughes, Julia Mattson, Margaret Cable, and Charles Grantier.[6] Joe was also instrumental in starting the First Annual Bowman Artists Guild Prize Exhibit.

Because of limited production with quality handwork of two people over a short period of time, Messer pottery is difficult to find. Such items as the mallard duck and Christmas bell are especially rare.[7] The mallard was particularly time-consuming, with much elaborate hand-painted detail. The porcelain Christmas bell was a personal gift to relatives and customers in 1953, with production limited to 50. Several pieces, which illustrate the creativity of Joe Messer as a potter, were never made to sell in quantity as they proved to be too labor intensive. These included a nude figurine, using an eight-piece mold; seahorse vase with design overlaid in a Wedgwood-type application; and an incised horse head vase. Vases with Sang-de-Boeuf (oxblood) glazes were difficult to make, requiring an extremely temperamental process.

North Dakotans, particularly local ranchers, have been collecting Messer pottery for some time. Perhaps the secret of the Messer success lies in Joe Messer's own aim, "to make the owner feel that here is his native soil brought into his house and made beautiful and useful by the skill of human hands."[8] Now the word is out, beyond state confines. Once people have seen and observed examples, they become captivated by the quality of the Messer creations.

Messer native clay, wheel-thrown stoneware. Courtesy of Eunice Messer.

Ceramics By Messer Marks

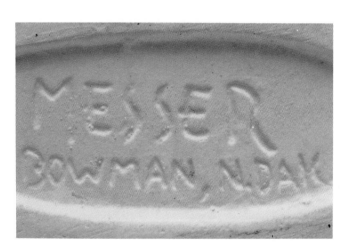

Naturalistic 3¾" x 5½" antelope on 4¾" x 5" ashtray, $350.00-400.00. (Private collection.)

Porcelain Hereford bull, 9¾" x 4½", modeled from a prize bull staked outside the studio window, $1,000.00+. (Private collection.)

1½" Christmas bell sent in 1953 as a Christmas card by Eunice and Joe, $200.00-300.00. (Private collection.)

Hereford family figurines, bull 3" x 4¾", $300.00-350.00; and cow 2" x 4½", $300.00 – 350.00. (Private collection.)

2¼" prairie dog figurines, $100.00 – 150.00 each. (Private collection.)

Hand-thrown 6¾" teapot, $200.00 – 250.00. Joe Messer was especially pleased with the spout. (Private collection.)

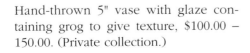

Paper attachment for hand-thrown items.

Hand-thrown 5" vase with glaze containing grog to give texture, $100.00 – 150.00. (Private collection.)

"Ceramics by Messer" trademark 3½" ashtray, $100.00-125.00.

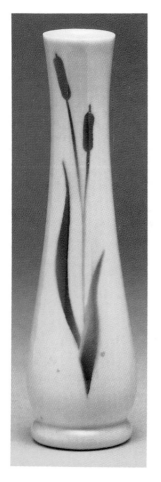

10" wheat vase with wheat motif in relief and airbrush shaded areas, $150.00 – 200.00. (Private collection.)

Porcelain 5" hand-painted bud vase, $125.00 – 150.00. (Private collection.)

Hand-thrown 4" flower pot with experimental glaze which bub-
bled when fired to produce lava effects, $50.00 – 75.00.

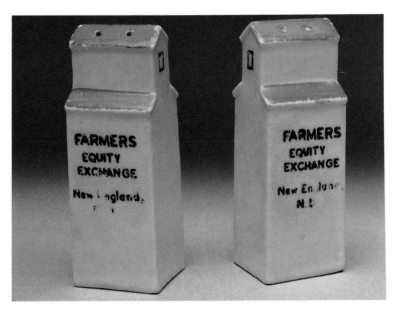

3½" grain elevator salt and pepper shaker
giveaways for company's best customers,
$100.00 – 150.00.

Turn, turn, my wheel! Turn round and round
Without a pause, without a sound;
So spins the flying world away!
This clay, well mixed with marl and sand,
Follows the motion of my hand;
For some must follow, and some command,
Though all are made of clay!

— H. W. Longfellow
Keramos

Rushmore Pottery

As Mount Rushmore is a symbol of our nation's determination to carve a democracy from the wilderness, so also its by-product, Rushmore Pottery, captures this nation's pioneering spirit. As a remote mountain was transformed into a majestic national monument, so ordinary clay was transformed into beautiful art pottery.

Mount Rushmore brought together two talented artisans who went on to create Rushmore Pottery; Ivan Houser, who studied sculpture and fine arts at the University of Oregon, and William Tallman, a New York City-trained sculptor. Both worked on Mount Rushmore for several years.

An early architectural influence and mentor of Ivan Houser was Dr. Avard T. Fairbanks, noted architect, who at age 21 was teaching his first University of Oregon class. Houser, 18, was in that class and continued his studies in sculpture and fine arts. Ivan Houser then worked as an architectural sculptor and modeler of terra cotta ornamental designs for the Northern Clay Company, Auburn, Washington. Continuing as an architectural sculptor for Gladding McBean and Company, Ivan's work enhanced buildings in San Francisco, Sacramento, Los Angeles, Salt Lake City, Houston, Seattle, and Portland.

After studying at the Art Students League, New York City, Ivan Houser was asked by Gutzon Borglum, main sculptor of the Mount Rushmore project, to be his assistant.

Ivan Houser had first become interested in pottery and glazes while working at Gladding McBean with terra cotta. Having had no formal classes in ceramics, Houser used his natural artistic ability, picking up knowledge and researching by himself, soon becoming prolific at the wheel.

Ivan Houser at homemade kiln. Courtesy of William and Peggy Tallman.

Driving between Rapid City and Mount Rushmore, Houser noticed a clay deposit along the highway. After cutting some clay from the bank and experimenting, Houser purchased thirteen acres of land, probably the first known commercial clay bed in the state.

William S. Tallman started his sculpting experience during summer vacation from high school when he lived with Gutzon Borglum and worked in his studio. After high school, Tallman studied art in New York City at the Grand Central School of Art and the Art Students League.

Working again for Borglum since 1928, Tallman was asked to work on Mount Rushmore in 1929. He was soon appointed superintendent in charge of all work on the memorial. Borglum described Tallman as a

William Tallman outside pottery workshop in woods. Courtesy of William and Peggy Tallman.

man "with considerable training in art and experience in studio work. He brings to his position as superintendent of the work an even temper, the gift of patience and sanity in judgment and appreciation of men."[1] Tallman found Borglum to be fascinating and an inspiration.

In their spare time and during periods when the Mount Rushmore project was shut down because of bad weather or lack of funds, Ivan Houser and William Tallman worked on creating what may be the first South Dakota pottery other than that made by the Native Americans. In a note to his son, Ivan Houser states, "I designed and made the first kiln — all the throwing and refining machinery, etc. It was crude in 'them thar days!'"[2] John Houser calls his father "a practical man, who grew up on a ranch and knew about things like blacksmithing and machinery. When he needed that first kiln, he built it."[3] Ivan Houser quit work on the monument in 1935 to devote full time to the pottery; William Tallman resigned in December of that year to join him, forming a successful partnership of good friends.

Permaclay was chosen as the first name of the pottery. However, this name was quickly changed to Rushmore as people thought they were using a special patented material and a question arose regarding previous right to the name.[4] Rushmore also gave better name identification.

Majestic woods, heavy and dark with towering ponderosa pines, enveloped the pottery workshop. William Tallman recalled "getting a shack and putting it up at Grizzly Gulch"[5] at the end of a narrow dirt road which turned off the main dirt road between Keystone and the Rushmore Monument.

Tallman also told of buying a log cabin for ten dollars and moving it log by log to a location beside the highway in Keystone. This log cabin became the salesroom.

According to Peggy Tallman, most pottery was sold to Mount Rushmore tourists. A family enterprise, the wives, Peggy Tallman and Mildred Houser, sold the wares. Peggy Tallman described the success of the three-month summer sales. "The pottery was not expensive but cost a lot for the times. We made enough money for two families to live on."[6]

Mount Rushmore not only brought the two principals together, but provided the sales potential for this pottery. From the start, Gutzon Borglum had anticipated that "millions of people would come here."[7] As Borglum stated about his choice of a remote area hidden from public view, "I knew that no matter where we carved, roads would be built and the public would find us."[8] Indeed, tourists started streaming in on gravel roads before the monument was completed. Rushmore Pottery capitalized by providing the tourists with souvenirs.

William Tallman did much of the marketing throughout the region, selling to retail stores. He said he would "find the best jeweler or gift shop in town and try to sell through them, giving exclusive sales rights for the area."[9]

The clay Houser had discovered was outstanding for making pottery. Mr. Tallman stated, "We didn't do a thing to it." The great plasticity of the clay made it unnecessary to add materials to form pottery and the finished pottery was extremely strong. Mr. Tallman tells of "throwing a pot across the room to show that it wouldn't break easily. Most shapes would ring like a bell when tapped, indicating they were well-fired."[10] Describing the quality of Rushmore ware, Ivan Houser stated that "the texture and character of the clay when fired makes for absolute unity between the body of the ware and the glaze, thus the absorption of moisture, chipping, and crazing is eliminated."[11]

Rushmore glazes adhere to the Charles Binns' philosophy that "much of the fascination of pottery making is centered in the glaze...because of the beauty and usefulness it imparts to ware."[12] Formulas from Binns'

Log cabin pottery salesroom in Keystone. Courtesy of William and Peggy Tallman.

book, *The Potters Craft,* were utilized, but Ivan Houser also fulfilled Binns' challenge to the craftsman — experimenting and creating his own glazes. Houser never purchased ready-made glazes. He created all his own glazes throughout the pottery's production.

Glazes used on Rushmore Pottery are widely diverse, ranging from crystalline to matte to high gloss in many colors and textures. Especially unique is the uranium glaze developed by Houser, a bright orange

which generates Geiger counter clicks. This glaze was discontinued during World War II as it was impossible to get the uranium material.

Rushmore crystalline glazes are reminiscent of nature's winter etchings, frost appearing on window panes. A striking "sunburst" crystalline effect was used occasionally. With their infinite shades and markings, even the potter doesn't know what variations will results from the crystalline firing process.

In rutile glazes, crystallization with a wide variety of streaked and mottled effects results from the combination of titanium dioxide with iron oxide. Rutile glazes allow the color of the clay body, which is fired brown, to partially show through, creating a mottling of the two colors.

After a first bisque-firing, most Rushmore pottery was sprayed with glaze and then refired. Little was dipped. The lead glazes required good exhaust ventilation. A second glazing, "repeat glazing" created flow effects.[13] Some pieces were sold in unglazed states.[14]

An early Rushmore sales brochure written by Ivan Houser as a marketing tool, delineates the company philosophy regarding molded ware. "Only shapes which because of their adaptability cannot be created on the potter's wheel, are made in molds. These pieces are first of all handmade with great study and care." More molded items, some appearing to be less carefully

Inside log cabin salesroom. Courtesy of William and Peggy Tallman.

Ivan Houser on a photo card advertising Permaclay Pottery.

designed, were made late in production. These included paperweights, western items like cowboy hats and boots, and figurines of people, animals, and birds.

Sitting Bull masks honored the famed Native American chief who defeated Custer and the white man at the Battle of Little Bighorn. The mask was modeled by Ivan Houser, with a Native American posing.[15]

Most Rushmore pottery is plain, emphasizing form and glaze. Decorative motifs are rare. Some sgraffito decorations used were zig zags, stars, plants, and horse heads. Art Deco reliefs appear on early tiles. Underglaze painting decorated some items, including figurines.

The simple yet sculptural forms of Rushmore Pottery reflected the backgrounds of both Houser and Tallman as sculptors, as well as the influence of Charles Binns. Like other artists of the period, they were trained in Binns' theories. According to William Tallman, "We used the Binns' book like a Bible." Ivan Houser's personal concepts of shapes which stressed the importance of scale and a structural philosophy dealing with intervals and proportions, sounds a great deal like that of Charles Binns' sense of form which includes "outline, proportion, structure."[16]

Most Rushmore products, although decorative, are useful. Houser felt that pottery must be "beautiful and useful at the same time," again echoing Binns' doctrine of "good, simple, utilitarian forms."[17] The majority seem to be vases, with pitchers also made in some quantity. Small pieces in the four to six inch range dominate, but pottery up to three feet high is known to have been produced.

Hand-thrown pottery was the focus of Rushmore. Ivan Houser worked like a studio potter, "being solely responsible for each object."[18] Houser followed the Binns' precept "control of the whole artistic process from conception to finished piece."[19] Occasionally a potter was hired to help, but Houser continued to do the vast majority of the hand throwing. William Tallman created many of the early tiles.

In 1940, Tallman sold his share of the pottery to Houser and left South Dakota. With the threat of war, the Tallmans realized that the tourist business would be ruined and felt that there would not be enough income to keep the company going.

Ivan Houser continued with the pottery until 1942. During these later years, more molded pieces were produced. A resident recalled that several Native Americans were working for Houser, as documented by their names appearing on some of these pieces.

In 1942, his mother's untimely death prompted Houser to move his family back to his aging father's ranch in Oregon. Ivan Houser sold the Rushmore Pottery inventory to Francis "Bud" Duhamel, who owned Duhamels Trading Post in Rapid City and pottery production ceased. The store, started by early Duhamel settlers, catered to the tourist trade. At that time, most of the inventory consisted of molded pieces. Duhamel said he didn't get the molds and didn't know what happened to them. Bud Duhamel had a kiln built above his store and planned to continue making pottery to sell. "We were already selling souvenirs. I thought we could also make and sell these."[20]

However, World War II stopped Duhamel's plans as he was unable to get help. Duhamel continued to sell the Rushmore inventory at this store, putting out a few pieces at a time until he closed his store in 1984. Items were sold with the original price tags and labels. Duhamel then sold Rushmore at Sitting Bull Crystal Cave until the stock was depleted in the late 80s.

It seems fitting that Bud Duhamel, grandson of a pioneer fur trader, followed the pioneer founders of Rushmore as owner. At age 87, Duhamel still led tours into the cave which had been purchased by his parents in 1929 before the road between Keystone and Mount Rushmore was built. Duhamel happily recalled watching the Sioux dance and perform their "Sitting Bull Sioux Indian Pageant" in front of the cave.

Regarding involvement Rushmore Pottery had with the other potteries of North and South Dakota, a short newspaper article told of William Tallman conferring at UND with Margaret Cable concerning pottery problems. A few of the Rushmore pieces resemble Cable's creations at the Dickinson Clay Products Company, but this may be coincidental. Also, Charles Grantier spent a month working at Rushmore pottery as a glazer in 1941.

In a 1936 Christmas letter to friends, Margaret Cable told of her summer swing around the Black Hills with Flora Huckfield. Near Keystone "it was great fun to watch the Rushmore potters at work in their little pottery on the side of the mountain under the shade of the pine trees. Lovely pottery they make, too, of a nearby clay — all thrown on the wheel."[21]

Pottery items acquired by Laura Taylor for her inspiration at Rosemeade are at the Richland County Historical Museum. Included in this display is a piece of Rushmore, signed "Ivan Houser 1941" in a uranium orange glaze.

Earliest pieces were marked "PERMACLAY." After the company name was soon changed to Rushmore Pottery, a black ink stamp or incised "Rushmore Pottery Black Hills S. D." was used. Some pieces were signed by Ivan Houser and dated. A few were signed by other potters. An occasional piece is marked "Guaranteed Handthrown." Paper labels appear to have been used only in the later years.

After leaving Rushmore and North Dakota, William Tallman worked for a Chattanooga, Tennessee, technical ceramics company for 30 years. Upon retiring, William and Peggy Tallman built a home in the Texas Hill Country and Tallman continued limited production of bronze sculptures.

Ivan Houser continued his pottery interest in the

Northwest. After founding the Colony Town Pottery, Aurora, Oregon, Ivan Houser made the pottery for three years. The Aurora Colony was an early commercial society settled in 1856 and disbanded in 1883. As tourists were attracted by its many preserved historic buildings, Aurora seemed an opportune place for a pottery. According to John Houser the pottery was not very successful. Oregon people weren't interested in buying pottery. Some was sold in California by a jobber, but California was already flooded with pottery at that time. Although Ivan Houser made all his own glazes, John stated that Aurora Colony pottery was more commercial, less artistic, and poorer quality than Rushmore pottery.

A creative bend runs in the family as generations of Housers have continued the artistic tradition. Ivan's mother, an amateur painter of some accomplishment, was very supportive of his work. Ivan's son, John, has become a prominent sculptor. John's son is also an artist.

Ivan Houser was creative in many spheres, not only art. For example, building a boat became a successful project. Other art media included drawing, watercolors, and oils. After guest lecturing at various colleges, Ivan Houser served 16 years as professor of ceramics, sculpture, and design at Lewis and Clark College, Portland, Oregon. While teaching, Houser created bronzes for himself and commemorative reliefs for a foundry in Portland. After retiring to California, Ivan Houser died in 1978.

The tie-in with Mount Rushmore has made this pottery more collectible. Mount Rushmore holds special meaning for Americans. This "Shrine of Democracy" sends a message as strong as its granite. The four United States presidents symbolize American ideals of freedom, justice, democracy, and independence. As South Dakota promotional material states, "Millions of Americans who stand in silence at the foot of Mount Rushmore see the hopes, dreams, determination, and will of a nation emblazoned in stone."[22]

The Rushmore potters themselves helped to carve this national treasure. Later, their pottery was part of the tourist experience of Mount Rushmore. The concepts of quality, endurance, values, and hard work evidenced in Mount Rushmore also endure in Rushmore pottery.

Because Rushmore pottery was sold to tourists from across the country, the pottery did not need to reflect local themes or interest. Instead, just as Teco and other forerunner potteries had relied on beautiful form instead of decoration, Rushmore appealed to those seeking the "simplicity of beautiful lines and colors."[23]

Selling primarily to tourists also meant wide distribution for Rushmore pottery. Because tourists carried this pottery to their homes throughout the nation, Rushmore is widely available now as a collectible.

Early Rushmore pottery with its original glaze formulations and hand craftsmanship displayed fine artistic qualities. Rushmore appeared in exhibitions in Syracuse, Cleveland, Philadelphia, and the Corcoran Gallery of Washington D.C. Early Rushmore was also made in limited quantities by the potters themselves. However, collectors should be aware that in the later years of the pottery, high quality often declined markedly as inexpensive molded items were produced.

The same concepts that helped Rushmore Pottery win its share in a highly competitive 1930s and 1940s market are key to Rushmore's collectability today — creativity, hand craftsmanship, and studio pottery ideals. Returning to arts and crafts philosophy, Ivan Houser believed that "Art pottery is not a passing fad, but a true and lasting art as can be evidenced by past history. Such art is not a product of a machine age any more than music or painting...It is the direct message of the artist wrought infinitely into his medium of expression from his own hand and brain."[24]

Rushmore Pottery Marks

Permaclay, first name used by Rushmore pottery, 2¼" sugar and creamer with clay showing through blue semi-gloss glaze, $250.00 – 300.00.

Permaclay mark.

Dealers sign, 3½" by 8½" of greenish gold glaze, $500.00+.

Striated pieces. 4½" pale blue pitcher, $65.00 – 85.00; 3¾" green vase, $50.00 – 75.00; 5¼" uranium glaze orange vase, $125.00 – 150.00.

Blue 6¼" pitcher, $40.00 – 50.00; light blue 4¾" pitcher, $40.00 – 50.00; 6" maroon vase, $40.00-50.00; 3¼" robin's egg blue vase, $35.00 – 45.00; 3¼" white vase, $35.00 – 45.00; 7" green pitcher with swirl, $50.00 – 60.00.

Early molded cast pieces. Stylized Art Deco floral mint green 5" trivet, designed by William Tallman, $125.00 – 150.00; 5" trivet in maroon, $125.00 – 150.00; 2¼" maroon paperweight with molded animal and star, $75.00 – 100.00; blue 3½" by 4½" ashtray with relief pine cone motif, $75.00 – 100.00.

Swirl 7" pitchers. Uranium orange, $125.00 – 150.00; green with blue highlights, $100.00 – 125.00; dark green, $100.00 – 125.00; yellow, $100.00 – 125.00.

Slip-painted cattails. Long 11" greenish white dish and 5" vase, $75.00 – 100.00 each.

Mark on long dish.

Blue 2" by 5½" sugar and creamer with molded decoration, $50.00 – 75.00; and maroon 1½" salt and pepper shakers on 6¼" base, $75.00 – 100.00.

Orange uranium glaze. 5½" swirl vase with gold streaks; 4¾" vase with turquoise interior and gold highlights, signed "Ivan Houser 41"; 1½" by 7½" bowl with turquoise interior, signed "Ivan Houser 41"; 6½" vase with gold highlights. $125.00 – 150.00 each.

5½" blue vase, $35.00 – 45.00; 3" oatmeal vase, $30.00 – 40.00; 3½" mint green vase, $35.00 – 45.00; 2½" pink handled vase, $45.00 – 55.00; 12½" maroon vase, $75.00 – 100.00; 8" pink double-handled vase, $50.00 – 75.00; 8" maroon double-handled vase, $50.00 – 75.00.

Rutile 4½" vase, $75.00 – 100.00; 6¾" uranium orange vase, $125.00 – 150.00; 3½" ruffled rutile vase, $75.00 – 100.00.

Green crystalline hand-thrown 6½" vase, $100.00 – 125.00.

Unusual glaze vases. 5" crystalline green; 4¾" flow green; 5½" crystalline green, 3½" flow green. $40.00 – 50.00 each.

4¾" aqua vase, $35.00 – 50.00; 2¾" aqua bowl, $25.00 – 40.00; 2" by 6" pink bowl with aqua interior, $25.00 – 40.00; 4" pink vase, $35.00 – 50.00.

Green vases all signed "Ivan Houser 41." 6" with brown streaks; 4½" banded vase; 5¼" with brown highlights, $40.00 – 55.00.

Decorative glaze pitchers. 4½" light blue streaked pitcher with brown interior and 4½" light blue pitcher with streaks in exterior and interior. $40.00 – 55.00 each.

Uranium orange 4" by 4½" vase, $100.00 – 125.00; 1½" by 4½" maroon bowl, $30.00 – 40.00; 3½" variegated blue vase, $35.00 – 55.00; 4½" green vase, $30.00 – 50.00.

Hand-thrown vases. 2½" maroon bowl; 5" matte maroon vase; 4¾" maroon vase; 5½" maroon vase; 2¾" pitcher, 4¾" gloss blue vase. $25.00 – 35.00 each.

Rutile 4½" handled vase, "Ivan Houser 41," $75.00 –
100.00.

Blue 3½" vase with concentric rings, $35.00 – 45.00; airbrush shaded white to blue 5½"
vase, $45.00 – 65.00; 2½" sugar and creamer with rings, $35.00 – 45.00.

Crystalline uranium 8¾" bowl, marked and dated "Ivan Houser 7/28/40," $150.00 – 225.00.

Ruffled hand-thrown vases. 4¾" crystalline green; 4¾" green streaked; 5" dark maroon; 4¼" light maroon; 4½" pink. $35.00 – 65.00 each.

Cowboy hats. Brown gloss glaze, 2¼" x 5¼"; maroon gloss glaze, 1¾" x 4"; brown gloss glaze, 5¼" x 2¼". $30.00 – 50.00 each.

Flower arrangers. Blue 3¼" vase, $25.00 – 35.00; 2¼" x 3½" turtle on base, like figurine with same mold, $25.00 – 35.00.

Sitting Bull mask, black gloss glaze, 6½" x 5½", $200.00 – 250.00. This mask, modeled by Ivan Houser, with a Native American friend posing, was purchased at Sitting Bull Cave.

Bisque, 2¾" vase; 4" trivet of man with stein; 3½" boots. $20.00 – 30.00 each.

Molded pieces. Aqua 3" vase; 7½" rose vase; blue 3" vase, aqua 4½" vase; maroon 4½" vase. $20.00 – 40.00 each.

Molded 3½" cowboy boots, $30.00 – 40.00 each.

Small molded pitchers, 1½" to 3", $20.00 – 30.00 each.

Figurines. Pink 3" x 4¾" burro; 2¼" pink owl; uranium orange turtle on base, 2¼" x 3½"; 2¼" tan owl; brown 3" x 4¾" burro; $50.00 – 75.00 each.

Hand-thrown pieces made by Rushmore employees. Aqua 4½" vase, marked "Blue-dog," $35.00 – 50.00; blue 5" vase, signed "Tony Lanz," $30.00 – 50.00; aqua 1¾" x 3½" bowl by "Bluedog," $25.00 – 35.00; dark pink 4¼" vase by Tony Lanz, $30.00 – 50.00.

Late molded 4¼" vases. Purple with brown flow; yellow with green flow; uranium orange with brown highlights. $20.00 – 30.00 each.

Late tiles/ashtrays, lighter in weight than those produced earlier. Maroon 4¼" x 5" ashtray; aqua 5" x 6" eagle tile; gold 4" trivet of man with stein; maroon 4¼" x 5" ashtray of Mount Coolidge; brown 5" x 5½" buffalo; $20.00 – 30.00 each.

Native American figurines. 6¼" standing, $80.00 – 100.00 each; 3½" to 4" smaller, $70.00 – 90.00 each.

3½" to 3¾" ashtrays, $20.00 – 30.00 each.

Late yellow molded 2¾" to 4" vases, $20.00 – 30.00 each.

Aurora Colony Town pottery made by Ivan Houser in Oregon after he left Rushmore. Maroon 2¾" bowl, $25.00 – 35.00; metallic green 9¼" pitcher, $50.00 – 60.00; maroon with flow white 5¾" vase, $40.00 – 50.00; striated 4½" green vase, $30.00 – 40.00.

Colony Town mark.

The earth gave forth her treasures.
We used them.
And beauty was begun.

I am a particle of the whole,
and yet another universe maintain.
Mingled galaxies
I contain…clay

one with the earth

Pine Ridge Pottery

Distinctive in design, unique in concept, high in quality — all are apt descriptions for Pine Ridge Pottery, a pioneering effort of Plains Native Americans. The history of Plains Native American pottery differs significantly from Southwestern Native American pottery, which has been a thriving business and collectible for decades. However, these Plains descendants of our first Americans also "took the mud from under tired feet, fashioned it into beauty with their hands and flung it to the stars making something of themselves and of their people."[1]

According to evidence at the North Dakota Heritage Center, Bismarck, North Dakota, pottery was already being made in the geographic area of the Dakotas in 400 B.C., continuing on until the later 1700s. Crescent-shaped tools, formed from buffalo scapulas, have been excavated. Orange stains and clay remnants on these tools indicate use in pottery making.

The Lakotas, recently made famous by the movie, *Dance with Wolves,* were historically nomads, carrying all their belongings on their backs and pursuing lives as hunters and gatherers. After the Native American uprisings and the demise of the buffalo, these Native Americans were confined to reservations and their nomadic existence ceased.

By 1890, the Pine Ridge Reservation had become the official headquarters for the Oglala Lakota tribe, also known as Sioux. The reservation spreads across nearly two million acres of Badlands in western South Dakota.

As the mid 1930s Work Progress Administration programs swept the nation, the growing economic importance of craft production by Southwestern Native Americans was recognized. Government officials began to encourage self-help developments in other Native American communities. Ceramic projects were introduced in the schools so that children on the reservations could make pottery for use in their homes.

Crude, black, pit-fired pottery was the first attempt at the Pine Ridge Boarding School on the Pine Ridge Reservation. The pottery, described as rough-textured, unfinished and not waterproof, was such poor quality that the students did not want to use it in their homes.[2]

Two people came to the Pine Ridge Reservation in 1937 and changed the course of events — Margaret Cable and Bruce Doyle. Cable, director of the University of North Dakota ceramics department, served as Traveling Educational Expert in Ceramics, Indian Service at Large for the United State Field Services. When Cable came to Pine Ridge for six months, she did not turn to Southwestern Native American traditions. Cable experi-

Bruce Doyle. Courtesy of Bruce Doyle, Jr.

mented with clay from the reservation and encouraged her students in the boarding school and summer school classes to use their own designs. Employees of the Indian Bureau of Affairs could take the summer school pottery making class for University of South Dakota credit to retain teaching certification. Elsie Bonser, a student in the class, expressed the esteem held for Margaret Cable, "She was a great person. We were all crazy about her."[3]

Bruce Doyle, ceramics director at Fort Yates (Standing Rock Reservation) was in Cable's class. Soon thereafter, William O. Roberts, superintendent of the Pine Ridge Reservation, and W.O. Nicholson, director of the boarding school educational program, were instrumental in bringing Doyle to Pine Ridge as director of the school pottery program. But Margaret Cable was his inspiration. According to Doyle's son, Bruce Doyle, Jr., "Maggie planted the seed of possibility. Margaret Cable was Dad's angel."[4]

Under Bruce Doyle's leadership, Pine Ridge Pottery became a successful enterprise at the Pine Ridge Boarding School. An insightful man, Doyle recognized the economic potential of pottery making. Doyle was a self-taught chemist who took ceramic classes at the University of Washington, University of California at Los Angeles, University of Oregon, and University of Wisconsin in Milwaukee. Having prepared his own glazes

Ella Irving.

at Fort Yates, Doyle compounded glazes compatible with the local Pine Ridge clay.

A perfectionist, Doyle would "cave it in, throw it on the wedging table and start over"[5] if a piece did not meet his standards. When satisfied with shapes created on the wheel, he would make molds so that items could be duplicated and produced more efficiently. Seconds weren't sold, but broken or given away.

An enterprising teacher, Doyle started the first adult classes for Native Americans at the school. One of his first students was Olive (Ollie) Cottier, who soon became very proficient in making pottery. Ella Irving, Olive's sister who had been working in Arizona for ten years, came home for a visit in 1939. Although she had become fascinated with the Hopi making pottery in Arizona, Ella did not learn how to make pottery while she was there.[6] With the opportunity to learn at Pine Ridge, Ella took a three month adult night class from Mr. Doyle and started making pottery. A third sister, Bernice Talbot, joined her two sisters in 1943. Although she received no formal training through classes, Talbot picked up the skills by "being there."[7] As Ella Irving stated, "Indian people are creative and good with their hands."[8]

An astute organizer, Doyle showed marketing and promotional flair. He blanketed South Dakota, networking for consignment places to sell Pine Ridge. He drove directly to gift shops in his car, pulling a trailer of goods behind. Duhamels Trading Post, Rapid City, South Dakota, and the famous Wall Drug Store in Wall, South Dakota, were two major outlets for Pine Ridge. The Rapid City Sioux Indian Museum shop also sold Pine Ridge pottery.

On the Pine Ridge Boarding School campus, an arts and crafts shop in a log cabin was opened to sell pottery, weaving, and crafts, such as leather work. Although the shop was open year round, most of the merchandise was sold to tourists in the summer. Pottery outsold weaving and other crafts. Both plain and decorated pieces sold well, with the decorated pieces costing a little more. Doyle's wife, Dorothy, who sold at the shop also described filling barrels of pottery for her husband to sell on his travels. "Small bowls and vases were the most popular because tourists could easily pack them in their luggage."[9]

A persistent man, the Native Americans gave Doyle the name "Charging Bear." Statistics provide a tribute to the success of Doyle's operation. When Doyle came in 1937, there was thirty dollars in the "Arts and Crafts" account. When Doyle left in 1942 for a promotion to principal of the American Horse Day School in Allen, South Dakota, this amount had grown to $40,000. In 1965 Doyle received the Distinguished Service Medal for his service to Native Americans from the United States Congress.

Apparently the pottery would have ceased production during the 1940s if it had not been for the Irving sisters. These three Lakota women continued to work at the school in the same room where classes were held. Occasionally, Ella and Olive taught. Olive is described by her sisters as the most artistic and gifted. Bernice's sense of humor and Ella's drive and spirit kept them going. They became self-directed. "We all helped each other and shared — that's an Indian tradition. We knew what to do and how hard we had to work to make ten dollars."[10]

Bernice tells of working from 8 a.m. to 5 p.m. and

Bernice Talbot.

then firing the kiln and staying until 2 a.m. Other nights, the sisters would haul the pottery home and continue into the night. "It was hard work. You made the whole thing, start to finish, from mixing the clay. Then you'd get ten-fifteen-twenty cents for a piece, but I enjoyed making pottery because you had something to show for what you did."[11]

At one time, Ella left Pine Ridge for six months to work in a Philadelphia factory. When she returned, Ella recounts that she "ran into the shop and stuck her hands into the clay. It was something you could conquer."[12]

Around 1953, Bill Artis, a Ph.D.-trained artist from the East, was hired as the new director at the school. With a specialty in sculpture and modeling, he marched to a different drum than did the Lakota. Artis attempted to make changes and introduce new concepts of modern art which failed. The sisters wanted to continue to make pottery as they had in the past, so all three quit.

During the same period, the Indian Bureau of Affairs decided to get out of the arts and crafts business. According to Harry Eagle Bull, Department of Education Bureau of Indian Affairs, there was "a general trend to do away with that kind of vocational curriculum."[13] Dorothy Field from Denver sold the remaining inventory at low prices and closed the shop.

In 1955 the stage was set for yet another Pine Ridge era when Ella Irving's determination paid off and she became an entrepreneur. The shy Ella credits Olive with "putting some fight in me." Obtaining a loan from her tribe, she purchased the pottery from the Pine Ridge Boarding School. Ella purchased kiln, wheel, formulas, molds, and all, starting production with her sister Bernice in a log cabin in downtown Pine Ridge.

In less than a year, Bernice moved to Rapid City and Ella was running the operation alone. Ella tells of hard times, working everyday, taking only Christmas and Easter off. Ella's love for pottery making never waned. "I loved my work. It was never off my mind what I wanted to make. I had to learn the business the hard way but I never tired of making pottery." Anticipation upon opening the kiln was a special joy, "a big surprise every time, to see how everything turned out. I feel I've accomplished something not everyone could do."[14]

The Source Directory of Native American Owned and Operated Arts and Crafts Businesses described Ella as the "sole producer of authentic Pine Ridge pottery, a sgraffito-decorated ware in buff-colored slip over red-brown clear glaze, employing traditional Sioux designs in various sizes of

Pine Ridge pottery.

bowls, vases, ashtrays and pitchers."[15] Ella marketed her product at her shop where more tourists came every year. She also sold through a Mount Rushmore gift shop and the Sioux Indian Museum shop in Rapid City. "It was all I could handle. I had no problem selling the pottery. My problem was filling the orders."[16] As the guiding light behind the continuation of Pine Ridge pottery, Ella Irving demonstrated pottery making several times at fairs and shows, including the Rapid City Range Days Fair. She was awarded first, second, and third for her exhibitions at the All American Indian Days in Sheridan, Wyoming. A one-person show featured Ella Irving's work at the U.S. Department of Interior Indian Arts and Crafts Board, Sioux Indian Museum and Crafts Center, Rapid City.[17] An annual series, the one-person exhibitions promote the creative work of individual Native Americans.

In the early 1980s, Ella's shop was vandalized and equipment stolen by locals. Even her award-winning ribbons were taken. This destruction of the facility made it impossible for Ella Irving, who still gets letters for orders, to continue and Pine Ridge ceased production.

Pine Ridge Reservation itself provided local red clay for the pottery. Dorothy Doyle remembered her husband coming home with great excitement in finding a clay bank that worked. Bruce Doyle Jr. describes his father "scrounging around to find clay pits. He would go out with a trailer and his own car to get it. Dad would taste the clay and grind it around in his mouth to check the quality."[18] Because of the high quality of these deposits, nothing needed to be added to the clay.

Doyle found the white clay used for the decoration in the Black Hills near Rapid City. Ella Irving continued to use these clay beds. Clay from the Black Hills seems fitting for this pottery. The Black Hills were called Paha Sapa (meaning Black Forest or Black Timber) by Native Americans and were considered closest to paradise, a dwelling place of beauty and peace. With their great regard for Mother Earth, Native Americans traditionally take only what is needed from the ground.

Both plain and decorated Pine Ridge pottery were made, each with its own unique characteristics. Less plain ware was produced than decorated, according to Ella Irving. With plain colored glazes, high firing caused the colored glazes to burn out irregularly to clear, thus highlighting the iron oxide of the red clay underneath, which imparts its own beauty. Bruce Doyle had been using these types of glazes at Fort Yates before coming to Pine Ridge.[19] Because commercial glazes were not compatible with the red clay — "like crayons not working on red paper" — Doyle's son stated that Doyle manufactured glazes for the clay.[20] Ivory, blue, green, and brown plain glazes were used. The glazes were sprayed until Ella's era, when the glazes were brushed on, as the spray was more wasteful and expensive.

Sgraffito, a carving technique, was the most common decorative technique. White clay slip on a red clay background was scratched off with a sharpened orange stick to create the design. Transparent glaze was then applied before the second firing. This technique, used so effectively by Margaret Cable in her University of North Dakota work, was also taught in her 1937 Pine Ridge class.[21] On the other decorated ware, the artist would incise the design into the red clay and apply a milky white glaze. This relationship of the design to the milky white glaze, through which it is revealed, has been described as "magical!"[22]

Designs of Pine Ridge pottery are Sioux motifs, very geometric, abstract, and angular as they were first used in quill and beadwork. The Sioux designs often depicted nature and tribe activities. Although some designs are symbolic for individual artists and may tell a story, symbolic language does not appear to be shared or interpreted universally within the tribe.[23]

Quill and Beadwork of the Western Sioux provides insights regarding the differing designs of Sioux men and women significant for Pine Ridge pottery. While the men used realistic figures, copying birds, animals, and people as accurately as possible, Sioux women used only geometric forms, including triangles, bands, and squares. The reason for this, practical or ceremonial, has not been discovered. However, you "can be sure of one thing in looking at any decoration by the Western Sioux: if it is geometrical in form...it was done by a woman."[24]

The designs, often based on intuition and carried in the memory of the artist, were done freehand and not drawn on first. Already in Cable's class, the students were encouraged to use their own ideas for designs. The resulting designs were a very significant feature of the pottery according to Evelyn Whirlwind Horse, a member of the first class.[25]

Both hand thrown and molded items were made at Pine Ridge, but molded pieces predominated because of cost savings. In making molded pieces, the seams were scraped off using the wheel of a pedal-swing machine and the top was cut off with an old crochet hook while the piece went around. Deep-sea sponges were also used for smoothing. According to Ella, polishing stones and coil ware, popular with Southwest Native Americans, were not used. The dense clay at Pine Ridge made processes required for coil ware and slabware methods too difficult.

Although now considered by many to be art forms, all Pine Ridge pottery was made for use, with a second firing making it both waterproof and oven proof. This utilitarian intent reflects the Native American attitude of use and preservation.[26]

A wide variety of items were made at Pine Ridge, including bowls, plates, teapots, water jugs, vases, mugs, ashtrays, pitchers, cups, and saucers. Cups, saucers, and plates were difficult to make. The handle had to be carefully applied to a cup. Saucers and plates tended to warp during firing because of the high iron content. Charles Binns, in *The Potter's Craft*, described the making of cups and saucers as the true test of a potter's skill.[27] Easier-to-make mugs replaced cups and saucers in 1943 and were very popular because they held heat well. In the history of Native American pottery making, change has always been the rule, as the art is not static but continually changing with the circumstances.[28]

The characteristic Pine Ridge mark was first used at the time the pottery became a commercial enterprise under Doyle. Variations of the mark, an incised pine tree and mountain with the name of the pottery and the artist's name, were used throughout the history of the pottery. "Indian" was part of the mark during the early period. Each artist drew their own mark, scratching it into the bottom while the piece was still damp.

A paper label was used by Ella Irving when her business expanded. Pottery bearing paper labels is also marked on the bottom with the characteristic mark.

It is possible to date some of the pottery by using artist names and tenure at Pine Ridge. Placing some of these dates concretely is difficult because of differences in the memories of principals and lack of documentation. However, if considered generally, the dates are still helpful. Olive Cottier was marking pottery from before 1939 to 1954 or 1955 with the mark "COTTIER." "TALBOT" appears on pottery made by Bernice from 1943 to 1955. Ella Irving used three names while at Pine Ridge. From 1939 to 1942, Ella marked her pieces "WOODY," her married name. "COX" from her second marriage, appears on Ella's pieces for three to four years in the 1940s. Returning to her maiden name, "IRVING" is Ella's signature during other time periods.

Other artist designations include "OGLALA," the mark of Bruce Doyle from 1937 to 1942, according to his son and wife. "NORA FIRETHUNDER," was a Native American woman friend of the Irving sisters, who worked at Pine Ridge from 1939 to 1941. "RAMONA WOUNDED KNEE" is the name used by Olive Cottier, who had a French married name, for a few years in response to a request for more "Indian-sounding names."[29]

Student names also appear on Pine Ridge pottery. "OCHS," for Oglala Community High School, is on some of the pots. OCHS is the same as Pine Ridge Boarding School. Students were boarded at the school because of transportation problems, with students scattered across the reservation.

Student pieces, made at the high school as art class assignments, were kept by the students and not sold in the Arts and Crafts Shop.[30] The only salable pieces were made by the adult women and approved by

Bruce Doyle in the early years. The women continued to make pottery to be sold in the shop after Doyle left, until the shop was closed.

Because there was no quality control of student work, student pieces vary widely in quality. Each must be considered on its own merit

Some of the Native Americans, trained in pottery making as students at the high school, came off the Pine Ridge Reservation and went to Rapid City. They worked in potteries like Lakota Pottery and Sioux Pottery. Some of these potteries were not Native American owned and operated and employed non-Native Americans. Branley Allen Branson in his Holiday 1975 article describes some of the pottery as "low-cost polychrome-on-white..I suspect a commercial process aimed at mass sales."[31] Much of this pottery continues to be made. Since this pottery was not made on the reservation and had different characteristics, it should not be considered Pine Ridge.

At least two Pine Ridge-trained students have gone on to make names for themselves in the pottery world. Len Randall continues to use techniques he learned at Pine Ridge as he works in California. His pieces, marked "Len Randall, Little Buffalo, Sioux," are difficult to confuse with Pine Ridge as they look so different. Al Blacktail Deer, featured in a 1975 U.S. Department of the Interior Indian Arts and Crafts Board one-person exhibition,[32] continues to make pottery in Rapid City.

Another Native American enterprise of the Dakotas — Three Tribes Stoneware, Inc. of New Town, North Dakota — is discussed in Appendix III.

Regarding collecting, "Today, American Indian art rides at the pinnacle of appreciation."[33] With increasing recognition of Native American arts and crafts as part of the rich diverse heritage of all Americans, demand for Native American pottery has soared. Renewed interest in Native American culture, art, and history is currently strong, as evidenced by record numbers of books being published in these areas.[34] The Civil Rights Movement of the 1960s brought new respect for minorities and greater appreciation for their contributions to our heritage. As Native American affairs have begun "to receive prominent national attention, the result has been an almost incredible increase in demand for fine Indian arts and crafts."[35]

During the Art and Crafts Movement of the early 1900s, American potters turned to their craft traditions, looking at Native American crafts, just as European potters had been inspired by Europe's medieval tradition. The simple, geometric designs and hand craftsmanship of Native American ware were considered appealing qualities and used in adaptations. Already in 1902, students in Charles Binns' classes were using Native American ware for designs.[36] Several potteries brought out lines using Native American designs during this time, including Clifton Art Pottery, Weller, and Rookwood.

Anita Ellis in *Rookwood Pottery: The Glorious Gamble* mentions incised Native American designs which "were probably discontinued sometime before 1915 when the vogue for all things Indian faded."[37] The recent revival of interest in arts and crafts furniture, metal, and pottery has renewed interest in Native American pottery.

Native American crafts created for the tourist trade have often been devalued with the implication that they are less authentic. However, arts and crafts cannot flourish unless they have an economic base as the craftsperson must be able to make a living by selling or trading items produced. Modern tourists and collectors serve the same function as ancient Southwestern traders. Trading of vessels stimulated excellence as the most artistic pieces were more in demand and disseminated further.[38] In a similar way, the tourist or collector provides financial support, which perpetuates craft production of quality ware. As Mark Bahti points out in *Southwestern Indian Arts and Crafts,* it is "the maker's intent" which determines "the integrity of the work," not whether the buyer is non-Native American.[39]

Pine Ridge pottery, an authentic Native American creation of remarkable artisans, is still often available at reasonable prices. The collecting of some authentic Native American artifacts, like beadwork, quill work, peace pipes, and feathered war bonnets has become limited on today's collector market as they are difficult to recognize and scarce.[40] Museums are also diminishing the supply of these available relics.

Pine Ridge is collectible for many of the same reasons that Southwestern Native American ware is collectible. The role of the individual artist has continued to rise as "individual artist-craftsmen take innovative approaches to contemporary art."[41] Pine Ridge is pottery made by individual artists with unique perspective. Current interior decorators search for the "ethnic idiom which shines forth."[42] With either its simplicity of beautiful lines and color or its sophisticated sgraffito decoration techniques, Pine Ridge fits into the aesthetic demands of today's contemporary market as well as the collectibles market. Hand craftsmanship and geometric design appeal to the public tastes. "The aesthetic appeal of . . . Indian pottery lies in sensing its earthy fragrance and most of all in associating the vessels with people, life, and the mystic roots of nature."[43]

When Margaret Cable and Bruce Doyle began to work with the Lakota, pottery was a new concept for the culture. As previously recognized with their quill beadwork, the "art style came naturally to the Sioux woman who passed white man's materials through an Indian's imagination."[44] Pine Ridge pottery was the artistic result of this interweaving of two cultures as the Irving sisters used their innate art sense and natural skills to create quality American art pottery.

Characteristic mark.

Paper sticker at time of Arts and Crafts Shop.

Paper sticker of Ella Irving's ownership era.

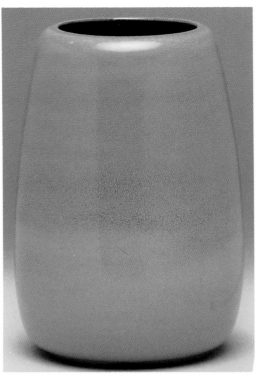

Mark of early vase.

Early airbrush shaded gloss glaze 7" vase, dated 1937, $400.00 – 500.00.

These UND glazes are like those used at Pine Ridge and most likely brought there by Margaret Cable. Brown 3" coiled vase, incised "SD-8" and UND blue seal, $50.00 – 75.00; 1¾" green flower bowl by Julia Mattson, $40.00 – 50.00; brown 3½" vase, incised "SD-8," $40.00 – 50.00.

Avocado green gloss glaze used at both UND and Pine Ridge. 2¼" x 7" bowl with Pine Ridge mark and "Reed," $40.00 – 50.00; 3½" vase marked with UND seal and "FLH" for Freida Hammers, $50.00 – 75.00.

Blue green 2" cup with 5½" saucer by Ella Cox, $50.00 – 75.00; green 3½" mug by Bernice Talbot, $30.00 – 50.00.

4¾" x 9¼" jardiniere with flowing glaze by Olive Cottier and marked "Sioux Indian," $400.00 – 500.00.

Large Cottier vases, with sgraffito cream-colored geometric motifs on red background under clear glaze. 7¼" x 5½" and 7¼" x 5"; $350.00 – 400.00.

Early geometric design serving set including 6½" x 10" pitcher with interesting spout and four 3½" tumblers, signed "Ramona Wounded Knee," $600.00+.

Incised geometrics under milky transparent glaze decorate this 3" x 6" tan bowl by Cottier, $300.00 – 350.00.

Large geometric motif. Bowl, 2" x 10" signed "N. FIRETHUNDER"; 10½" plate by "B. Talbot"; $300.00 – 350.00 each.

Deep blue plain gloss glaze. 2¾" x 4" bowl, signed "Ramona W. Knee," $50.00 – 75.00; 2½" vase by Nora Firethunder, $40.00 – 50.00; Cottier 3¾" vase, $40.00 – 50.00; 4½" x 6¾" Ella Irving bowl, $75.00 – 100.00.

Geometric 7" star-motif plate by Irving, $200.00 – 250.00; and geometric 2" x 2¾" Cox salt and pepper shakers, $75.00 – 100.00.

6" incised geometric vase by Cottier, $300.00 – 350.00.

Salt and pepper shakers. 2½" geometric by Talbot, $75.00 – 100.00; 2¼" light green by Talbot, $25.00 – 35.00; 2" green by Talbot, $25.00 – 35.00; 2" x 3" white by Cox, $25.00 – 35.00.

2½" vase by Firethunder and 1¼" x 4" bowl signed "Woody"; $100.00 – 125.00 each.

Metallic sheen. 2½" vase, described by Ella Irving as an "end of the month vase" made from a combination of left-over glaze filings, signed "Woody," $200.00 – 250.00.

Geometric design. Irving 6½" vase, $225.00 – 250.00; Talbot 1¼" x 2½" dish, $75.00 – 100.00; Cottier 3¾ vase, $125.00 – 150.00; Irving 3¾" vase, $150.00 – 175.00; Cottier 5½" vase, $175.00 – 200.00.

Hanging basket, 5" x 7½", with geometric design by Woody, $250.00 – 300.00.

White plain glaze. 4½" vase by Cottier; 4¾" pitcher by Firethunder; 3½" pitcher by Cottier; Woody 3½" vase; Talbot 4¼" tumbler; 4¾" tumbler; $30.00 – 50.00 each.

Incised with green highlights. 4½" Cottier vase, $200.00 – 225.00; 2½" vase with artist name obscured by glaze, $125.00 – 150.00; 2¾" x 5½" Firethunder bowl, $200.00 – 225.00.

3½" x 2¼" sugar and 3" creamer by Cottier and 2¼" sugar and creamer by Talbot, $125.00 – 150.00 each set.

White 2" sugar and 3" creamer by Cottier and aqua 2" sugar and 2½" creamer by Irving, $50.00 – 75.00 each set.

Geometric dinnerware. 7¼" Irving pitcher, $175.00 – 200.00; 3½" Irving mug, $75.00 – 100.00; 3¼" Cox mug, $75.00 – 100.00; 4¼" Talbot tumbler, $75.00 – 100.00; 5½" Woody tumbler, $75.00 – 100.00.

Geometric sgraffito light green design on 4¼" vase by Woody, $125.00 – 175.00.

Geometric bowls; 1½" x 5½" Irving; 3¼" x 5½" Irving; 2¾" x 7½" Irving; $125.00 – 150.00 each.

Shades of lighter blue. 4½" vase by Cottier, $40.00 – 60.00; 2½" Firethunder vase, $30.00 – 50.00; 3½" Cottier pitcher, $40.00 – 50.00; 4" Cottier pitcher, $40.00 – 60.00.

Green glaze tea set by Cox with 7½" teapot, 2" sugar, and 2½" creamer, $200.00 – 250.00.

Small geometric vases. 5½" Cottier vase; 3½" Cottier vase; 2¼" Woody vase; 3½" Cox vase; $100.00 – 125.00.

Green glaze. 7" Talbot vase, $50.00 – 75.00; 3¼" Irving vase, $30.00 – 40.00; 3" Irving vase, $30.00 – 40.00; 9¼" Woody vase, $60.00 – 85.00; 7" Talbot vase, $40.00 – 65.00.

2½" x 4¾" bowl with incised motifs and milky white glaze by Cottier, $250.00 – 300.00.

Geometric bowls. 2" x 9" by Cottier, $125.00 – 150.00; 2½" x 4½" signed "Ramona Wounded Knee," $100.00 – 125.00; 2¼" x 5¼" by Nora Firethunder, $125.00 – 150.00.

Green with brown showing through glaze, all by Cottier. 5" bulbous pitcher, $50.00 – 65.00; 4" vase, $40.00 – 50.00; 4" pitcher, $30.00 – 50.00; 3½" pitcher, $30.00 – 50.00; 6¼" pitcher, $50.00 – 60.00.

Predominantly brown glaze. 3½" Cottier vase, $35.00 – 55.00; 2" x 3" bowl by Cottier, $30.00 – 40.00; bowl, 3¼" x 4¾", by Cox, $40.00 – 60.00.

Rust gloss glaze, 4½" pitcher signed "N. FIRETHUNDER 80," $50.00 – 65.00.

Brown gloss glaze incised 2¼" x 5½" bowl by Olive Cottier, $250.00 – 275.00.

Geometric motif ashtrays. 1¼" x 4" with obscured artist mark; Nurses' Home Cheyenne River, 1" x 4¾" by Woody; 2" x 3¾" by Cottier; 1½" x 4¾" by Talbot, $75.00 – 100.00 each.

Plain glaze ashtrays. Green 1½" x 4¾" by Talbot; white, ¾" x 4¼" by Cottier; white, 1¾ x 4¼" by Talbot; white, 1½" x 4¾" by Talbot, $25.00 – 50.00 each.

Three 5½" geometric design plates by Cottier with differing variations of the same design, $100.00 – 150.00.

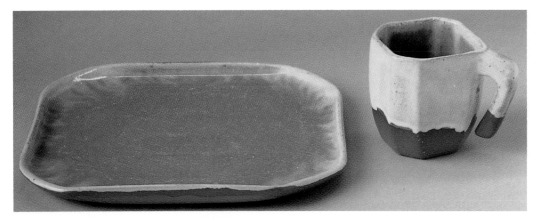

Restaurant ware made by Ella Irving for a Rapid City restaurant in the late 40's. 8¼" x 7¼" turquoise plate, $50.00 – 75.00; 3" mug of gray drip over red clay with turquoise interior, $50.00 – 75.00.

More restaurant ware with white flow edges on red clay. Tray 5¾" x 7", turquoise, $40.00 – 50.00; turquoise platter, 9" x 10½", $60.00 – 70.00; chartreuse dish, 1½" x 6", $40.00 – 50.00; turquoise tray, 5½" x 9¼", $40.00 – 50.00.

Candle Light restaurant ware mark.

White glaze 2" sugar and 2½" creamer by OCHS students, $50.00 – 75.00.

Sugar/creamer mark.

Student pieces. 2¾" x 5¼" bowl marked only "Pine Ridge 1/28, 38 Ro" and 3" x 3¼" vase with applied decoration, marked "Pine Ridge S. D. No. 16 Opal Hodges Mar. 6 40"; $75.00 – 100.00 each.

Pottery by Len Randall. 4¼" vase with black sgraffito made at Pine Ridge while a student, $75.00 – 100.00; current 2½" red and white vase, marked "Len Randall Little Buffalo Sioux," $20.00 – 30.00; current 2¼" green and brown on white clay piece, $20.00 – 30.00; 3¼" geometric design vase made while Pine Ridge student, $75.00 – 100.00.

Pottery by Al Blacktail Deer, all made after he left the Pine Ridge Reservation, all marked "WHEEL THROWN." 4½" vase dated 2/24/78, $30.00 – 40.00; 3" mug with cobalt blue sgraffito, $20.00 – 30.00; 9" pitcher with sgraffito Native American chief "VER. PAWNEE LEGGINGS," $50.00 – 60.00.

Indianesque motifs used by other potteries. Rookwood 3½" x 5½" bowl made in 1901, $150.00 – 200.00; 8" Rookwood 1910 vase, artist signed William Hentschel, $250.00 – 300.00; Weller Souevo ware 5" vase, $75.00 – 100.00; Clifton 3½" vase marked "FOUR MILE RUN 210," $150.00 – 175.00.

CONCLUSION

Women have served a dual role in the success of all the North and South Dakota potteries. First and foremost, women have been the primary consumers of decorative arts. "Women provided the market...for centuries in western society."[1] As homemakers, women usually make the decisions and are the purchasers of furnishings, including ceramics. By their economic clout, women, through their purchases, determine what will succeed. As women turned to the potteries of this Dakota region when creating their home environments, these potteries succeeded.

Women were also the primary creative force behind several of the potteries. The influence of Margaret Cable is far-reaching into most of the potteries. The women instructors/artists of the University of North Dakota, Laura Taylor Hughes of WPA and Rosemeade, and the Native American women potters of Pine Ridge were all major players.

Just as the buying public dictated the styles of art pottery when produced, so collectors in their collecting trends also influence today's collectible market. Several trends encompass art pottery of the Dakotas. General interest in various areas of collecting is growing. As more people are "cocooning," they "fill their homes with things that they think will make them happy."[2] With life becoming more complicated, people seek simple, naturalistic objects. As British master craftsman William Morris counseled, "Have nothing in your home that you do not know to be useful or believe to be beautiful."[3] Today's collectors are "attracted to the things that are handmade, reek of tradition and might increase in value."[4] Margaret Cable's qualities of "technically excellent and artistically pleasing" place most of the Dakota art pottery in this classification. Collectors are also returning to local art. Regional artists and designers are going to be increasingly attractive to collect as they become recognized.[5]

Several of the North Dakota potteries followed an American art pottery tradition of using local flora and fauna designs. The buying public identifies with these motifs, wherein lies their appeal. Already starting with John Ruskin, a British arts and crafts leader, natural designs were stressed instead of historical forms.[6] Ellsworth Woodward felt that art pottery "should be representative of the life of the people and the background of the section of which they live."[7] Therefore, Newcomb College moved from austere abstracted designs to naturalistic romantic images, which were more marketable. California pottery decorations were "modeled from life," with, for example, "lichens as lifelike as if just gathered from some old stone wall."[8] The Rookwood Pottery also used familiar plants for decoration. In North Dakota pottery as well, the native flora and fauna, part of the natural heritage of the area, provided "humanity with a measure of tranquillity and serenity that enriches our lives — ennobles the spirit."[9]

The potteries of North and South Dakota promote identity with heritage by portraying Dakota's legends, land, and people. Collectors enhance their own self-concepts by preserving the stories of these pioneer crafts people who wrote pages of Dakota history in enduring clay.

APPENDIX I

Hughes Fine Arts Center
University of North Dakota
Grand Forks, North Dakota 58202

J. Lloyd Stone Alumni Center
University of North Dakota
Grand Forks, North Dakota 58202
(701) 777-2611

North Dakota Heritage Center
612 East Boulevard
Bismarck, North Dakota 58505
(701) 328-2666

Pioneer Trails Regional Museum
100 E. Second Street, P. O. Box 1044
Bowman, North Dakota 58623
(701) 523-3600

Richland County Historical Museum
Second Street and Seventh Avenue North
Wahpeton, North Dakota 58075
(701) 642-3075

APPENDIX II

North Dakota Pottery Collectors Society
(An organization formed to promote pottery made in the state,
with a newsletter, annual convention, and commemorative.)
Sandy Short, Membership Chair
Box 14
Beach, North Dakota 58621

North Dakota Pottery Collectors Society commemoratives. 1994 Rosemeade-type sign, 1¾ x 4", $50.00 – 75.00; 1992 UND-type coyote 2¾" paperweight, $30.00 – 55.00; 1993 Dickota-type 4" incense burner, $25.00 – 35.00; 1991 paperweight, 3¼" x 2", decorated with prairie roses and wheat, $20.00 – 35.00.

Dickota brown gloss glaze 3¾" x 4" buffalo paperweight, $150.00 – 200.00. (Courtesy of Bill Vasicek collection.)

1995 Dickota-type 3½" x 3½" buffalo North Dakota Pottery Collectors Society commemorative, $15.00 – 25.00.

APPENDIX III

Three Tribes Stoneware Inc., New Town, North Dakota, had been an earlier amalgamation of three Native American tribes from the Missouri Valley — Mandan, Arikara, and Hidatsa. In the mid 1960s, federal Rural Area Redevelopment grant money trained Three Tribes potters on the Fort Berthold Reservation in west central North Dakota.

James Walker, a Wisconsin native, was recruited from the University of Wisconsin-Whitewater to be the professional potter in charge. Walker's first problem was "interesting local Indian women in the project and he finally talked ten into trying their hand."[1] Walker ended up with three whom he described as "the most skilled potters you'll find anywhere"[2] — Mary Elk, Emmaline Blake, and Sadie Youngbear.

Originally starting with Dickinson clay, the pottery was soon buying clay more suitable for its ware from Kentucky and Ohio, continuing use of local clay for color.

According to Emmaline Blake, one of the three original potters, hand throwing on the potter's wheel was emphasized.[3] Utilitarian products included pencil pots, ashtrays, cookie jars, vases, candle holders, hanging planters, wine goblets, and dinnerware. Walker stated that the potters spent "sixty per cent of their time turning out the bread-and-butter pots and the rest in exploring their personal ingenuity and creativeness to make some truly beautiful pieces."[4]

By 1971, four professional potters and two apprentices were employed as production increased. The stoneware was marketed in Colorado, South Dakota, North Dakota, Minnesota, Wisconsin, and Illinois. Emmaline Blake cited exhibitions in Rapid City, South Dakota; Washington D.C. and at the University of Minnesota, Minneapolis. However, the company went out of business in the 1970s. According to Marilyn Hudson, board of directors, two pieces of Three Tribes Pottery are on display at the Three Affiliated Tribes Museum on the Fort Berthold Reservation.[5]

The appearance and character of Three Tribes pottery differ markedly from Pine Ridge. As stoneware, Three Tribes is fired to a high temperature of 2,380°, resulting in complete vitrification and a dense body. Three Tribes has a contemporary look, not using the Native American geometric designs and sgraffito techniques of Pine Ridge. Walker explained why Three Tribes does not "look like Indian pottery...We're trying to take an old, fine, stagnant craft, and by modernizing it, make it useful to today's world."[6]

Three Tribes contemporary 3½" brown tumbler with concentric circles, $20.00 – 30.00; matte green 5" vase, $20.00 – 30.00; matte blue and white 3½" bird, $20.00 – 25.00.

Three Tribes mark.

END NOTES

UNIVERSITY OF NORTH DAKOTA POTTERY

1. Louis Geiger, University of the Northern Plains (Grand Forks, North Dakota: University of North Dakota Press,1958), 71.
2. "State Has Extensive Clay Deposits of Value," Grand Forks Herald (February 11, 1923).
3. "Cable pottery: UND's unique tie to the earth of Dakota," Alumni Review (January, February 1994), 8.
4. Margaret Cable, personal papers on file at the Elwyn B. Robinson Department of Special Collections, Chester Fritz Library, University of North Dakota, Grand Forks, North Dakota. Many of the quotes and much of the information about Margaret Cable are from these personal papers.
5. Margaret Cable, letter to Bertha R. Palmer, undated.
6. Cable, letter to Palmer.
7. Margaret Cable, personal letter, November 25, 1912, to Thomas B. Anderson, M. Knowles Pottery Company, East Liverpool, Ohio.
8. John E. Howard, letter to John Rogers, Dean of the College of Fine Arts, University of North Dakota, October 26, 1977.
9. Cable, personal papers.
10. "Margaret Cable Chosen to Represent North Dakota at Famous Women's Fair," Grand Forks Herald (May 15, 1927) 10.
11. Margaret Cable, "Potters In Action — Come To See Them on Engineers' Day," Ceramic Department Open House Invitation, undated.
12. Bertha Palmer, Beauty Spots in North Dakota. (Boston: The Gorham Press, 1928), 241.
13. Palmer, 241.
14. Cable, personal papers.
15. Hildegarde Fried Dreps, letter to author, September 3, 1976. Most information regarding Hildegarde Fried is derived from several interviews in person and written correspondence.
16. Hildegarde Fried Dreps, interview.
17. Dreps, interview.
18. Milton B. Larson, Dean of the College of Engineering, personal letter, January 18, 1967.
19. Larson, letter.
20. Howard, letter
21. Howard, letter.
22. Freda Hammers Rich, telephone interview.
23. Cable, personal papers.
24. Freida Hammers Rich, letter to author, July 7, 1976.
25. Margaret Pachl, interview.
26. Dreps, interview.
27. Scott H. Nelson, "Two UND Artists," North Dakota Pottery Collectors Society Newsletter, Vol. 3, Number 2 (April 1993,) 7.
28. Papers on file at the Elwyn B. Robinson Department of Special Collections, Chester Fritz Library, University of North Dakota Grand Folks, North Dakota.
29. Dreps, interview.
30. Cable, personal papers.
31. Judson T. Webb, Pottery Making (Chicago: Lewis Institute, 1914), 18.
32. "Art Workers: Minnesota Women in the Arts and Crafts Movement," an exhibition at the James J. Hill House, Minnesota Historical Society, St. Paul, Minnesota, April 16 – September 24, 1994.
33. "Design 1880 – 1945: The Modern Idiom," exhibition, the Wolfsonian Foundation, Miami Beach, Florida, January 1995.
34. Cable, personal papers.
35. Margaret Cable, "North Dakota Pottery," North Dakota Club Bulletin (April 1927.)
36. Margaret Cable, paper on "Post-War Ceramic Opportunities in North Dakota," undated.
37. Paul B. Kannowski, Wildflowers of North Dakota (Grand Forks, North Dakota: University of North Dakota Press, 1989), 7
38. Margaret Cable, "Featuring North Dakota Industries," Great Northern Semaphore, Vol. 4 (June 1927), 5.
39. Cable, personal papers.
40. Cable, "Post-War Ceramic Opportunities."
41. Margaret Kelly Cable, "Pottery from North Dakota Clays," brochure (Grand Forks, North Dakota: University of North Dakota Division of Mines, Circular Number 1, December 15, 1926).
42. Freida Hammers, "Bentonite In Ceramic Decoration," abstract presented at the North Dakota Academy of Science, Fargo, North Dakota, 1932, 5.
43. Hammers, abstract, 5.
44. W. E. Budge, "Ceramics in North Dakota," North Dakota Engineer (May 1936), 4.

45. Elizabeth Cumming and Wendy Kaplan, The Arts and Crafts Movement (London: Thames and Hudson, Ltd., 1991), 131.
46. Rich, correspondence.
47. Margaret Cable, letter to Edward C. Papin, The Conde Naste Publications, New York City, March 5, 1930.
48. Cable, personal papers.
49. M. Beatrice Johnstone, "Nodak Clay Valuable for Pottery," The U. N. D. Alumni Magazine (July 1927), 15.
50. Cable, pesonal papers.
51. William McKenney, paper on "The Clay Resources of North Dakota," 1952.
52. Louis C. Harrington, Dean of the College of Engineering, personal letter, May 25, 1949.
53. "American Pottery," exhibition announcement, undated.
54. William G. Whitford, "Ceramic Art at a Century of Progress Exhibition," School Arts (October 1933), 99.
55. Cable, "Post-War Ceramic Opportunities."
56. Rich, interview.
57. Margaret Libby Barr; Donald Miller and Robert Barr, University of North Dakota Pottery: The Cable Years (Fargo, North Dakota: Knight Printing Co., 1977), 38 – 51.

DICKINSON CLAY PRODUCTS COMPANY — DICKOTA POTTERY

1. Bobbie Forester, "Workers in Clay," Arkansas Gazette (September 11, 1932), 5.
2. Howard Lewis, interview. Much factual information in this chapter came from interviews with Howard Lewis.
3. "Dickinson Firm Makes First Bid for Foreign Markets for Pottery Manufactured from North Dakota Clays," Mandan Evening Pioneer (August 24, 1935).
4. Mandan Evening Pioneer, August 24, 1935.
5. James R. Gilbert, Through Minnesota's Seasons with Jim Gilbert (Minneapolis, Minnesota: Minnesota Landscape Arboretum, 1987), 195.
6. "The Story of Dickota Pottery," brochure, Dickinson: North Dakota Herald, undated.
7. Marion John Nelson, Art Pottery of the Midwest (Minneapolis, Minnesota: University Art Museum, 1988), 74.
8 Howard Lewis, letter to Dorothy Bigwood, State Library Commission, Bismarck, North Dakota, Febuary 16, 1953.
9. Mandan Evening Pioneer, August 24, 1935.
10. Nelson, 74.
11. Lois Lehner, Lehner's Encyclopedia of U. S. Marks on Pottery, Porcelain and Clay (Paducah, Kentucky: Collector Books, 1988), 319.
12. Anita J. Ellis, Rookwood Pottery: The Glorious Gamble (New York: Rizzoli International Publications, Inc., 1992), 15.
13. Arkansas Gazette, 5.
14. Jessie Poesch, Newcomb Pottery: An Enterprise for Southern Women, 1985-1940 (Exton, Pennsylvania: Schiffer Publishing, Ltd., 1984), 66.
15. Martin Eidelberg, "Myths of Style and Nationalism: American Art Pottery at the Turn of the Century," The Journal of Decorative and Propaganda Arts, Vol. 20 (1994) 97.
16. Eidelberg, 111.
17. Dickota Glaze Book, Elwyn B. Robinson Department of Special Collections, Chester Fritz Library, University of North Dakota, Grand Forks, North Dakota.
18. Nelson, 74.

WPA CERAMICS

1. Elaine Levin, The History of American Ceramics (New York: Henry N. Abrams, Inc., 1988), 147.
2. Levin, 147.
3. "Ceramics Development Project Finds Ready Response Here; WPA Has Charge; Make Many Articles," The Dickinson Press and Recorder-Post (September 10, 1936).
4. "Ceramics Department project finds ready response here."
5. Margaret Cable, personal papers on file at the Elwyn B. Robinson Department of Special Collections, Chester Fritz Library, University of North Dakota, Grand Forks, North Dakota.
6. Cable, personal papers.
7. Freida Hammers Rich, written correspondence to author.
8. Sharon Huxford and Bob Huxford, The Collectors Encyclopedia of Roseville Pottery (Paducah, Kentucky: Collectors Books, 1989), 64.
9. Garth Clark, American Ceramics 1876 to the Present (New York: Abbeville Press,1979), 263.
10. Levin, 148.

11. Lois Lehner, Lehner's Encyclopedia of U. S. Marks on Pottery, Porcelain and Clay (Paducah, Kentucky: Collector Books, 1988), 528.
12. Susan N. Cox, "The WPA Produced More Than Wages," Journal of the American Art Pottery Association, Vol. 1 (March-April 1985) 10.
13. Roy Nuhn, "Nursery Rhymes," The Antique Trader (March 8, 1995), 21.
14. Barbara Perry, Editor, American Ceramics: the Collection of Everson Museum of Art (New York: Rizzoli International Publications, Inc., 1989), 123.
15. Paul S. Dornhauser, History of American Ceramics: The Studio Potter (Dubuque, Iowa: Kendall/Hunt Publishing Company, 1978), 88.

WAHPETON POTTERY COMPANY — ROSEMEADE POTTERY

1. Erling Nicolai Rolfsrud, Extraordinary North Dakotans (Alexandria, Minnesota: Lantern Books, 1954), 199.
2. Freida Hammers Rich, letter to author, July 21, 1976.
3. Laura Taylor, letter of October 21, 1940, on file at the Richland County Historical Museum.
4. Howard Lewis interview.
5. "Seven Hundred Women Attend Pottery Open House," Richland County Farmer-Globe (October 22, 1940), 1.
6. Rolfsrud, 202.
7. Papers on file at the Richland County Historical Museum.
8. Phil Penas, "North Dakota Clay Used in Wahpeton Pottery Business," Fargo Forum (May 31, 1953), 22.
9. Laura Taylor Hughes, "The Potter's Art," North Dakota Horticulture (January 1947), 11.
10. Penas, 22.
11. Penas, 22.
12. Hughes, North Dakota Horticulture, 11.
13. Marion John Nelson, Art Pottery of the Midwest (Minneapolis, Minnesota: University Art Museum, 1988), 75.
14. "Birdies Sing in New Designs," Richland County Farmer-Globe (November 13, 1951).
15. Federal Workers Project, North Dakota: A Guide to the Northern Prairie State (Oxford, England: Oxford University Press, 1950), 175.
16. Josa Keyes, The Teddy Bear Story (New York: Gallery Books, 1985), 8.
17. 1947 newspaper on file at Richland County Historical Museum.
18. "Souvenir Birds Prove Popular with Hunters," Richland County Farmer-Globe (November 6, 1945), 1.
19. Penas, 22.
20 "Authentic Ceramic Fish Modeled at Pottery Here," Richland County Farmer-Globe (March 17, 1953), 9.
21. 1947 newspaper.
22. Mike Schneider, The Complete Salt and Pepper Shaker Book (Atglen, Pennsylvania: Schiffer Publishing, Ltd., 1993), 9.
23. Schneider, 154.
24 Leo A. Borah, "North Dakota Comes into Its Own," National Geographic Magazine (September 1951), 307.
25. Mary Stoudt, "Rosemeade," North Dakota Horizons, Vol. 9 (Spring 1979), 22.
26. "Rosemeade Potteries Is New Name for Local Pottery," Richland County Farmer-Globe (February 10, 1953), 2.
27. Joe McLaughlin, in person interview, telephone interview, and correspondence. Much information regarding this era is from Joe McLaughlin.
28. McLaughlin, interview.
29. McLaughlin, interview.
30. McLaughlin, interview.
31 Penas, 22.
32. McLaughlin, interview.
33. Betty McLaughlin, interview.
34. Shirley Sampson and Irene J. Harms, Beautiful Rosemeade (Garretson, South Dakota: Sanders Printing Company, 1986), 7.
35. "Wahpeton Only Place in Nation Selling Rosemeade Seconds," Richland County Farmer-Globe (May 1, 1953).

CERAMICS BY MESSER

1. Erling Nicolai Rolfsrud, Extraordinary North Dakotans (Alexandria, Minnesota: Lantern Books, 1954), 187.
2. Editor, "Pottery in the Chicken Coop," GTA Digest (November 1952), 21.
3. Eunice Messer, interview. Much factual information, as well as quotes in this chapter, came from interviews with Eunice Messer.
4. Messer, interview.
5. Messer, interview.

6. "American Art Week Show," exhibition catalog, Bismarck, North Dakota, November 1 – 4, 1951.
7. Les Snavely, museum director of Pioneer Trails Regional Museum, "Letter to the Editor," North Dakota Pottery Collector's Society Newsletter (April 1993), 6.
8. Rolfsrud, 192.

RUSHMORE POTTERY

1. "W. S. Tallman, Sculptor," brochure, undated.
2. Ivan Houser, personal papers.
3. John Houser, interview.
4. Peggy Tallman, telephone interview.
5. William Tallman, telephone interview.
6. Peggy Tallman, interview.
7. Edwald Hayes, interview.
8. "Mount Rushmore," Traveler Magazine (Summer 1989), 67.
9. William Tallman, interview.
10. William Tallmen, interview.
11. Ivan Houser, personal papers.
12. Charles F. Binns, The Potter's Craft (New York: D. Van Norstrand Company, Inc., 1910), 84.
13. William Tallman, interview.
14. Peggy Tallman, interview.
15. John Houser, interview.
16. Binns, X.
17. Editor, Design/Keramic Studio, Vol. 36 (January 1935), 16.
18. Janet Kardon, Editor, The Ideal Home 1900-1920: The History of Twentieth Century Craft in America (New York: Harry N. Abrams, Inc., 1993), 79.
19. J. F. Mahon, "Charles Fergus Binns," American Ceramic Society Bulletin, Vol. 17 (1938), 175.
20. Francis Duhamel, interview.
21. Margaret Cable, personal papers.
22. "South Dakota: Mount Rushmore and Crazy Horse," brochure, undated.
23. "New Uplift to American Pottery," The World's Work Advertiser (August 1904), 5.
24. Ivan Houser, "Rushmore Pottery from the Black Hills of South Dakota," sales brochure, undated.

PINE RIDGE POTTERY

1. "Clay, Water and Fire," exhibition catalog, An Exhibition of Southwest Pottery Yesterday and Today, Dahl Fine Arts Center, Rapid City, South Dakota, January – February, 1980.
2. Bruce Doyle, Jr. interview.
3. Elsie Bonser, interview.
4. Doyle, interview.
5. Doyle, interview.
6. Ella Irving, interview. Much information and several quotes come from interviews with Ella Irving.
7. Bernice Talbot, interview.
8. Irving, interview.
9. Dorothy Doyle, interview..
10. Talbot, interview.
11. Talbot, interview.
12. Irving, interview.
13. Harry Eagle Bull, telephone interview, Department of Education Bureau of Indian Affairs, Aberdeen, South Dakota.
14. Irving, interview.
15. Source Directory: Native American Owned and Operated Arts and Crafts Businesses (Washington, D. C.: Indian Arts and Crafts Board, U. S. Department of the Interior, 1980 – 81 Edition), 20.
16. Irving, interview.
17. "Pottery by Ella Irving," exhibition catalog, Rapid City, South Dakota: U.S. Department of the Interior Arts and Crafts Board, Sioux Indian Museum and Crafts Center, 1975.
18. Doyle, interview.
19. Doyle, interview.
20. Doyle, interview.
21. Evelyn Whirlwind Horse, telephone interview.
22. Marion John Nelson, Art Pottery of the Midwest (Minneapolis, Minnesota: University Art Museum, 1988), 80
23. Carrie A. Lyford, Quill and Beadwork of the Western Sioux (Boulder, Colorado: Johnson Books, 1989), 76.

24. Lyford, 13.

25. Whirlwind Horse, interview.

26. Beatrice Levin; Ruth F. Kneitel and Marjorie Vandervelde, Art of the American Indian (Billings, Montana: Montana Indian Publications, 1973), 14.

27. Charles F. Binns, The Potter's Craft (New York: D. Van Norstrand Company, Inc., 1910), 76.

28. Mark Bahti, Southwestern Indian Arts and Crafts (Las Vegas, Nevada: K C Publications, Inc., 1983), 40.

29. Talbot, interview.

30. Irving, interview.

31. Branley Allen Branson, "Hands Across the Plain," Holiday, Vol. 56 (March 1975), 33.

32. "Pottery By: Al Blacktail Deer," exhibition catalog, Rapid City, South Dakota: U. S. Department of the Interior Arts and Crafts Board, Sioux Indian Museum and Crafts Center, 1975.

33. one with the earth, U. S. Department of the Interior, The Institution of American Indian Arts, 1976, 5.

34. Alan Patureau, "Interest in American Indians is rising in publishing circles," Minneapolis Star Tribune (December 1, 1994), 8.

35. Francis Harlow, Modern Pueblo Pottery (Flagstaff, Arizona: Northland Press, 1977), 10.

36. Janet Kardon, Editor, The Ideal Home 1900-1920: The History of Twentieth Century Craft in America (New York: Harry N. Abrams, 1993), 85.

37. Anita J. Ellis, Rookwood Pottery: The Glorious Gamble (New York: Rizzoli International Publications, Inc.,1992), 53.

38. Harlow, 10.

39. Bahti, 3.

40. Stanley L. Baker, "Collecting the American Indian on Antiques," The Antique Trader (April 9, 1974), 42.

41. one with the earth, 6.

42. one with the earth, 9.

43. Harlow, vii.

44. Lyford, 86.

CONCLUSION

1. Ellen Paul Denker, "Women in the Arts and Crafts Movement: Artists, Consumers, Pioneers," Arts and Crafts Quaterly, Vol. 7, No. 1, 30.

2. Mary Abbe, "Belleek collectors like china with an Irish lilt," Minneapolis Star Tribune (March 16, 1995), 2.

3. "Art Workers: Minnesota Women in the Arts and Crafts Movement," brochure, An Exhibition at the James J. Hill House, Minnesota Historical Society, St. Paul, Minnesota, April 16 – September 26, 1994.

4. Abbe, 2.

5. Ann Wright, "A Classic Comeback," Collector (June 1994), 29.

6. Jessie Poesch, Newcomb Pottery: An Enterprise for Southern Women, 1895-1940 (Exton, Pennsylvania: Schiffer Publishing Ltd., 1984), 21.

7. Poesch, 66.

8. Kenneth R. Trapp, The Arts and Crafts Movement in California: Living the Good Life (New York: Abbeville Press Publisher, 1993), 132.

9. Paul B. Kannowski, Wildflowers of North Dakota (Grand Forks, North Dakota: University of North Datota Press, 1989), 1.

APPENDIX III

1. Cabe Dickey, "New Town Indians Are Busy Making Lots of Pot," Bismarck Tribune (November 13, 1968), 1.

2. Dickey, 1.

3. Emmaline Blake, Three Tribes potter, telephone interview.

4. Dickey, 2.

5. Marilyn Hudson, Board of Directors, Three Affiliated Tribes Museum, telephone interview.

6. Duane Lillehaug, "Three Tribes Begin New Tradition in Indian Pottery," reprinted in North Dakota Pottery Colletors Society Newsletter (February, 1993), 5.

BIBLIOGRAPHY

Abbe, Mary. "Belleek collectors like china with an Irish lilt," *Minneapolis Star Tribune*, March 16, 1995, pp. 128.

American Art Week Show, Bismarck, North Dakota, November 1–4, 1951, exhibition catalog.

"American Pottery," exhibition announcement, undated.

"Art Workers: Minnesota Women in the Arts and Crafts Movement," An Exhibition at the James J. Hill House, Minnesota Historical Society, St. Paul, Minnesota, April 16–September 24, 1994.

"Authentic Ceramic Fish Modeled at Pottery Here," *Richland County Farmer-Globe*, March 17, 1953, page 9.

Bahti, Mark. *Southwestern Indian Arts and Crafts*. Las Vegas, Nevada: K C Publications, Inc. 1983.

Baker, Stanley L. "Collecting the American Indian on Antiques," *The Antique Trader*, April 9, 1974, pp. 40 – 44.

Barr, Margaret Libby; Donald Miller, and Robert Barr. *University of North Dakota Pottery: The Cable Years*. Fargo, North Dakota: Knight Printing Co., 1977.

Barr, Paul E. *North Dakota Artists*. Grand Forks, North Dakota: University of North Dakota Library, 1954.

Binns, Charles F. *The Potter's Craft*. New York: D. Van Norstrand Company, Inc., 1910.

"Birdies Sing in New Designs," *Richland County Farmer-Globe*, November 13, 1951.

Borah, Les A., "North Dakota Comes Into Its Own," *National Geographic Magazine,* September 1951, pp. 283 – 322.

Branson, Branley Allen. "Hands Across the Plain," *Holiday*, Volume 56, Number 2, March, 1975, page 33.

Budge, W. E. "Ceramics in North Dakota," *North Dakota Engineer*, May, 1936, pp. 4 – 5.

Cable, Margaret. Personal letter to Edward C. Papin, The Conde Naste Publications, New York, New York, March 5, 1930.

____."Featuring North Dakota Industry," *Great Northern Semaphore*, Volume 4, Number 6, June 1927.

____."North Dakota Pottery," *North Dakota Club Bulletin*, April 1927, page 5.

——.Paper on "Post-War Ceramic Opportunities in North Dakota," undated.

——.Personal letter on November 25, 1912, to Thomas B. Anderson, M. Knowles Pottery Company, East Liverpool, Ohio.

——.Personal papers on file at the Elwyn B. Robinson Department of Special Collections, Chester Fritz Library, University of North Dakota, Grand Forks, North Dakota.

____."Potters In Action — Come to See Them on Engineers' Day," Ceramic Department Open House invitation, undated.

——. "Pottery from North Dakota Clays," brochure, Grand Forks, North Dakota: University of North Dakota Division of Mines, Circular Number 1, December 15, 1926.

"Cable pottery: UND's unique tie to the earth of Dakota," *Alumni Review,* January – February, 1994, pp. 8 –9.

Clark, Garth. *American Ceramics 1876 to the Present*. New York: Abbeville Press, 1979.

"Clay, Water and Fire," exhibition catalog. An Exhibition of Southwest Pottery Yesterday and Today, Dahl Fine Arts Center, Rapid City, South Dakota, January – February, 1980.

Cox, Susan N. "The WPA Produced More Than Wages," *Journal of the American Art Pottery Association,* Volume 1, Number 2, March – April, 1985, pp. 3 and 13 – 14.

Cumming, Elizabeth and Wendy Kaplan. *The Arts and Crafts Movement*. London: Thames and Hudson, Ltd., 1991.

Denker, Ellen Paul. "Women In the Arts and Crafts Movement: Artists, Consumers, Pioneers," *Arts and Crafts Quarterly,* Volume 7, Number 1, pp. 30 – 33.

Derwick, Jenny B. and Mary Latos. *Dictionary Guide to United States Pottery and Porcelain*. Franklin, Michigan: Jenstan, 1984.

"Design 1880 – 1945: The Modern Idiom," exhibition. The Wolfsonian Foundation, Miami Beach, Florida, January 1995.

Design/Keramic Studio, Volume 36, January 1935, page 16.

Dickey, Cabe. "New Town Indians Are Busy Making Lots of Pot," *Bismarck Tribune,* November 13, 1968, pp. 1 – 2.

"Dickinson Firm Makes First Bid for Foreign Markets for Pottery Manufactured from North Dakota Clays," *Mandan Evening Pioneer,* August 24, 1935.

Dickota Glaze Book. Elwyn B. Robinson Department of Special Collections, Chester Fritz Library, University of North Dakota, Grand Forks, North Dakota.

Dornhauser, Paul S. *History of American Ceramics: The Studio Potter*. Dubuque, Iowa: Kendall/Hunt Publishing Company, 1978.

Eidelberg, Martin. "Myths of Style and Nationalism: American Art Pottery at the Turn of the Century," *The Journal of Decorative and Propaganda Arts*, Volume 20, 1994, pp. 84 – 111.

Ellis, Anita J. *Rookwood Pottery: The Glorious Gamble*. New York: Rizzoli International Publications, Inc., 1992.

Evans, Paul. *Art Pottery of the United States*. New York: Feingold and Lewis Publishing Corporation, 1987.

Federal Writers Project. *North Dakota: A Guide to the Northern Prairie State*. Oxford, England: Oxford University Press, 1950.

Forester, Bobbie. "Workers in Clay," *Arkansas Gazette,* September 11, 1932, page 5.

Geiger, Louis. *University of Northern Plains*. Grand Forks, North Dakota: University of North Dakota Press, 1958.

Gilbert, James R. *Through Minnesota's Seasons with Jim Gilbert*. Minneapolis, Minnesota: Minnesota Landscape Arboretum, 1987.

Hammers, Freida L. "Bentonite In Ceramic Decoration," abstract presented at the North Dakota Academy of Science, Fargo, North Dakota, 1932.

Harlow, Francis. *Modern Pueblo Pottery*. Flagstaff, Arizona: Northland Press, 1977.

Harrington, Louis C., Dean of the College of Engineering, personal letter, May 25, 1949.

Houser, Ivan. "Rushmore Pottery From the Black Hills of South Dakota," sales brochure, undated.

Houser, John and Nicholas Houser. "Biographical Sketch of Ivan Houser, Sculptor and Ceramist June 29, 1901 – November 28, 1978," 1978.

Howard, John E., letter to John Rogers, Dean of the College of Fine Arts, University of North Dakota, October 26, 1977.

Hughes, Laura Taylor. "The Potter's Art," *North Dakota Horticulture*, January 1947, page 11.

Huxford, Sharon and Bob Huxford. *The Collector's Encyclopedia of Roseville Pottery*. Paducah, Kentucky: Collector Books, 1989.

Johnstone, M. Beatrice. "Nodak Clay Valuable for Pottery," *The U.N.D. Alumni Magazine,* July, 1927, pp. 14 – 15.

Kannowski, Paul B. *Wildflowers of North Dakota*. Grand Forks, North Dakota: University of North Dakota Press, 1989.

Kardon, Janet, Editor. *The Ideal Home 1900-1920: the History of Twentieth Century Craft in America*. New York: Harry N. Abrams, 1993.

Keyes, Josa. *The Teddy Bear Story*. New York: Gallery Books, 1985.

Larson, Milton B., Dean of the College of Engineering, personal letter, January 18, 1967.

Lehner, Lois. *Lehner's Encyclopedia of U. S. Marks on Pottery Porcelain and Clay*. Paducah, Kentucky: Collector Books, 1988.

Levin, Beatrice; Ruth F. Kneitel, and Marjorie Vandervelde. *Art of the American Indian*. Billings, Montana: Montana Indian Publications, 1973.

Levine, Elaine. *The History of American Ceramics*. New York: Henry N. Abrams, Inc. 1988.

Lewis, Howard, letter to Dorothy Bigwood, State Library Commission, Bismarck, North Dakota, February 16, 1953.

Lillehaug, Duane. "Three Tribes Begin New Tradition in Indian Pottery," reprinted in *North Dakota Pottery Collectors Society Newsletter,* February, 1993, page 5.

Lyford, Carrie O. *Quill and Beadwork of the Western Sioux*. Boulder, Colorado: Johnson Books, 1989.

Mahon, J. F. "Charles Fergus Binns," *American Ceramic Society* Bulletin, Volume 17, 1938, page 175.

"Margaret Cable Chosen to Represent North Dakota at Famous Women's Fair," *Grand Forks Herald,* May 15, 1927, page 10.

McKenney, William, paper on "The Clay Resources of North Dakota," 1952.

"Mount Rushmore," *Traveler Magazine,* Summer, 1989, page 67.

Nelson, Scott H. "Two UND Artists," *North Dakota Pottery Collectors Society Newsletter*, Volume 3, Number 2, April 1993, page 7.

Nelson, Marion John. *Art Pottery of the Midwest*. Minneapolis, Minnesota: University Art Museum, 1988.

"New Uplift to American Pottery," *The World's Work Advertiser,* August, 1904, page 5.

one with the earth. U. S. Department of the Interior, The Institute of American Indian Arts, 1976.

Palmer, Bertha. *Beauty Spots in North Dakota*. Boston: The Gorham Press, 1928.

Patureau, Alan. "Interest in American Indians is rising in publishing circles," *Minneapolis Star Tribune,* December 1, 1994, pp. 8–9.

Penas, Phil. "North Dakota Clay Used In Wahpeton Pottery Business," *Fargo Forum,* May 31, 1953, page 22.

Perry, Barbara, Editor. *American Ceramics: The Collection of Everson Museum of Art*. New York: Rizzoli International Publications, Inc., 1989.

Poesch, Jessie. *Newcomb Pottery: An Enterprise for Southern Women, 1895-1940*. Exton, Pennsylvania: Schiffer Publishing, Ltd., 1984.

"Pottery By: Al Blacktail Deer," exhibition catalog, Rapid City, South Dakota: U. S. Department of the Interior Arts and Crafts Board, Sioux Indian Museum and Crafts Center, 1975.

"Pottery of Ella Irving," exhibition catalog. Rapid City, South Dakota: U. S. Department of the Interior Arts and Crafts Board, Sioux Indian Museum and Crafts Center, 1975.

Rich, Freida Hammers, letter to author, July 7, 1976.

Rolfsrud, Erling Nicolai. *Extraordinary North Dakotans*. Alexandria, Minnesota: Lantern Books, 1954.

"Rosemeade Potteries Is New Name for Local Pottery," *Richland County Farmer-Globe,* February 10, 1953, page 2.

Sampson, Shirley and Irene J. Harms. *Beautiful Rosemeade*. Garretson, South Dakota: Sanders Printing Company, 1986.

Schneider, Mike. *The Complete Salt and Pepper Shaker Book*. Atglen, Pennsylvania: Schiffer Publishing, Ltd., 1993.

"Seven Hundred Women Attend Pottery Open House," *Richland County Farmer-Globe.* October 22, 1940, page 1.

Snavely, Les, museum director of Pioneer Trails Regional Museum, "Letter to the Editor," *North Dakota Pottery Collectors Society Newsletter,* Volume 3, Number 2, April, 1993, page 6.

Source Directory: *Native American Owned and Operated Arts and Crafts Businesses*. Washington, D. C.: Indian Arts and Crafts Board, U. S. Department of the Interior, 1980 – 81 Edition.

"South Dakota: Mount Rushmore and Crazy Horse," brochure, undated.

"Souvenir Birds Prove Popular with Hunters," *Richland County Farmer-Globe,* November 6, 1945, page 1.

"State Has Extensive Clay Deposits of Value," *Grand Forks Herald,* February 11, 1923, page 1.

Stoudt, Mary. "Rosemeade," *North Dakota Horizons,* Volume 9, Number 2, Spring, 1979, pp. 22 – 23.

"The Study of Dickota Pottery," brochure, Dickinson, North Dakota: North Dakota Herald, undated.

Trapp, Kenneth R. *The Arts and Crafts Movement in California: Living the Good Life*. New York: Abbeville Press Publishers, 1993.

"Wahpeton Only Place in Nation Selling Rosemeade Seconds," *Richland County Farmer-Globe,* May 1, 1953.

Webb, Judson T. Pottery Making. Chicago: Lewis Institute, 1914.

Whitford, William G. "Ceramic Art at a Century of Progress Exhibition," *School Arts,* October, 1933, pp. 99 – 106.

Wissinger, Joanna. *Arts and Crafts Pottery and Ceramics*. San Francisco: Chronicle Books, 1994.

"WPA Has Charge; Make Many Articles," *The Dickinson Press and Recorder-Post,* September 10, 1936.

Wright, Ann. "A Classic Comeback," *Collector,* June, 1994, pp. 25 – 30.

"W. S. Tallman, Sculptor," brochure, undated.

INTERVIEWS

Blake, Emmaline, North Dakota, by telephone June 1995.

Bonser, Elsie, Rapid City, South Dakota, in person October 1989.

Doyle, Bruce Jr., Taos, New Mexico, in person April 1991 and by telephone 1990 – 1991.

Doyle, Dorothy, Taos, New Mexico, in person April 1991.

Dreps, Hildegarde Fried, Maryville, Missouri, in person July 1975, April 1976, August 1976, November 1977, and several telephone interviews.

Duhamel, Francis, Rapid City, South Dakota, in person October 1989 and by telephone March 1990.

Eagle Bull, Harry. Aberdeen, South Dakota, by telephone February 1991.

Hayes, Edwald, Keystone, South Dakota, in person April 1989 and October 1989.

Houser, John, El Paso, Texas, in person September 1990 and several telephone interviews.

Hudson, Marilyn, New Town, North Dakota, by telephone June 1995.

Ingvalson, Clara, Ellendale, North Dakota, in person August 1977 and several telephone interviews.

Irving, Ella, Pine Ridge Indian Reservation, Pine Ridge, South Dakota, in person April 1989 and October 1989 and several telephone interviews.

Lewis, Howard, Wahpeton, North Dakota, in person August 1972, June 1989, October 1990, and several telephone interviews.

Messer, Eunice, in person August 1994, January 1995, and June 1995.

McLaughlin Betty, Arizona, in person November 1995.

McLaughlin, Joe, Arizona, in person November 1995 and by telephone March 1995 and June 1995.

Pachl, Margaret, Eureka Springs, Arkansas, in person August 1976.

Rich, Freida Hammers, Yucaipa, California, by telephone several times 1972 – 1977.

Talbot, Bernice, Rapid City, South Dakota, in person April 1989 and October 1989 and by telephone.

Tallman, Peggy, Ingram, Texas, by telephone several times 1990 – 1995.

Tallman, William, Ingram, Texas, by telephone several times 1990 – 1995.

Whirlwind Horse, Evelyn, Martin, South Dakota, by telephone April 1991.

About the Author

Realizing that soon the voices of the 1930s to 1950s pottery principals would be lost, Darlene Hurst Dommel began gathering their stories over twenty-five years ago. Several of these personal interviews form the basis of this book, recording their stories for posterity.

As a free-lance writer with a research-oriented master of science degree, Darlene Dommel has had over fifty magazine articles published in the antiques field, including the first nationally published articles on eight potteries.

Index

COLLECTOR BOOKS

Informing Today's Collector

For over two decades we have been keeping collectors informed on trends and values in all fields of antiques and collectibles.

The following is a partial listing of our books on pottery, porcelain, and figurines:

Blue and White Stoneware-McNerney-5½x8½-152 Pgs.-(PB) ....#1312/$ 9.95

Blue Ridge Dinnerware, Revised 3rd Ed.-Newbound-8½x11-160 Pgs.-(PB) ....#1958/$14.95

Blue Willow, Revised 2nd Ed.-Gaston-8½x11-169 Pgs.-(HB) ....#1959/$14.95

Collectible Vernon Kilns-Nelson-8½x11-256 Pgs.-(HB) ....#3816/$24.95

Collecting Yellow Ware-McAllister-8½x11-128 Pgs.-(HB) ....#3311/$16.95

Collector's Ency. of American Dinnerware-Cunningham-8½x11-322 Pgs.-(HB) ....#1373/$24.95

Collector's Ency. of Blue Ridge Dinnerware-Newbound-8½x11-176 Pgs.-(HB) ....#3815/$19.95

Collector's Ency. of California Pottery-Chipman-8½x11-160 Pgs.-(HB) ....#2272/$24.95

Collector's Ency. of Colorado Pottery-Carlton-8½x11-168 Pgs.-(HB) ....#3811/$24.95

Collector's Ency. of Cookie Jars-Roerig-8½x11-312 Pgs.-(HB) ....#2133/$24.95

Collector's Ency. of Cookie Jars, Vol II-Roerig-8½x11-400 Pgs-(HB) ....#3723/$24.95

Collector's Ency. of Cowan Pottery-Saloff-8½x11-176 Pgs.-(HB) ....#3429/$24.95

Collector's Ency. of Early Noritake-Alden-8½x11-216 Pgs.-(HB) ....#3961/$24.95

Collector's Ency. of Fiesta-Huxford-8½x11-190 Pgs.-(HB) ....#2209/$19.95

Collector's Ency. of Flow Blue China-Gaston-8½x11-160 Pgs.-(HB) ....#1439/$19.95

Collector's Ency. of Flow Blue China, 2nd Edition-Gaston-8½x11-184 Pgs.-(HB) ....#3812/$24.95

Collector's Ency. of Hall China, 2nd Edition-Whitmyer-8½x11-272 Pgs.-(HB) ....#3813/$24.95

Collector's Ency. of Homer Laughlin China-Jasper-8½x11-208 Pgs.-(HB) ....#3431/$24.95

Collector's Ency. of Hull Pottery-Roberts-8½x11-207 Pgs.-(HB) ....#1276/$19.95

Collector's Ency. of Lefton China-DeLozier-8½x11-144 Pgs.-(HB) ....#3962/$19.95

Collector's Ency. of Limoges Porcelain, 2nd Ed.-Gaston-8½x11-224 Pgs.-(HB) ....#2210/$24.95

Collector's Ency. of Majolica-Katz-Marks-8½x11-192 Pgs.-(HB) ....#2334/$19.95

Collector's Ency. of Metlox Potteries-8½x11-344 Pgs.-(HB) ....#3963/$24.95

Collector's Ency. of McCoy Pottery-Huxford-8½x11-247 Pgs.-(HB) ....#1358/$19.95

Collector's Ency. of Niolak-Gifford-8½x11-256 Pgs.-(HB) ....#3313/$19.95

Collector's Ency. of Nippon Porcelain I-Van Patten-8½x11-222 Pgs.-(HB).....................#3837/$24.95

Collector's Ency. of Nippon Porcelain, 2nd Series-Van Patten-8½x11-256 Pgs.-(HB)..........#2089/$24.95

Collector's Ency. of Nippon Porcelain, 3rd Series-Van Patten-8½x11-320 Pgs.-(HB)...........#1665/$24.95

Collector's Ency. of Noritake-Van Patten-8½x11-200 Pgs.-(HB) ....#1447/$19.95

Collector's Ency. of Noritake, 2nd Series-Van Patten-8½x11-264 Pgs.-(HB) ....#3432/$24.95

Collector's Ency. of Occupied Japan, Vol. I-Florence-8½x11-108 Pgs.-(PB)...................#1037/$14.95

Collector's Ency. of Occupied Japan, Vol. II-Florence-8½x11-112 Pgs.-(PB) ....#1038/$14.95

Collector's Ency. of Occupied Japan, Vol. III-Florence-8½x11-144 Pgs.-(PB) ....#2088/$14.95

Collector's Ency. of Occupied Japan, Vol. IV-Florence-8½x11-128 Pgs.-(PB) ....#2019/$14.95

Collector's Ency. of Occupied Japan, Vol. V-Florence-8½x11-128 Pgs.-(PB) ....#2335/$14.95

Collector's Ency. of Pickard China-Reed-8½x11-336 Pgs.-(HB) ....#3964/$24.95

Collector's Ency. of R.S. Prussia, 1st Series-Gaston-8½x11-216 Pgs.-(HB) ....#1311/$24.95

Collector's Ency. of R.S. Prussia, 2nd Series-Gaston-8½x11-230 Pgs.-(HB) ....#1715/$24.95

Collector's Ency. of R.S. Prussia, 3rd Series-Gaston-8½x11-224 Pgs.-(HB) ....#3726/$24.95

Collector's Ency. of R.S. Prussia, 4th Series-Gaston-8½x11-288 Pgs.-(HB) ....#3877/$24.95

Collector's Ency. of Roseville Pottery-Huxford-8½x11-192 Pgs.-(HB) ....#1034/$19.95

Collector's Ency. of Roseville Pottery, Vol. 2-Huxford-8½x11-207 Pgs.-(HB) ....#1035/$19.95

Collector's Ency. of Russel Wright Designs-Kerr-8½x11-192 Pgs.-(HB) ....#2083/$19.95

Collector's Ency. of Sascha Brastoff-Conti, Bethany, Seay-8½x11-320 Pgs.-(HB)...............#3965/$24.95

Collector's Ency. of Van Briggle Art Pottery-Sasicki & Fania-8½x11-144 Pgs.-(HB)..............#3314/$24.95

Collector's Ency. of Wall Pockets-Newbound-8½x11-192 Pgs.-(HB) ....#4563/$19.95

Collector's Ency. of Weller Pottery-Huxford-8½x11-375 Pgs.-(HB) ....#2111/$29.95

Collector's Guide to Country Stoneware & Pottery-Raycraft-5½x8½-160 Pgs.-(PB) ....#3452/$11.95

Collector's Guide to Country Stoneware & Pottery, 2nd Series-Raycraft-8½x11-375 Pgs-(PB)..#2077/$14.95

Collector's Guide to Harker Pottery-Colbert-8½x11-128 Pgs.-(PB) ....#3433/$17.95

Collector's Guide to Hull Pottery, The Dinnerware Lines-Gick-Burke-8½x11-168 Pgs.-(PB)..#3434/$16.95

Collector's Guide to Lu-Ray Pastels-Meehan-8½x11-160 Pgs.-(PB) ....#3876/$18.95

Collector's Guide to Made in Japan Ceramics-White-8½x11-214 Pgs.-(PB) ....#3814/$18.95

Collector's Guide to Rockingham-Brewer-5½x8½-128 Pgs.-(PB) ....#4565/$14.95

Collector's Guide to Shawnee Pottery-Vanderbilt-8½x11-144 Pgs.-(HB) ....#2339/$19.95

Cookie Jars-Westfall-5½x8½-160 Pgs.-(PB)..#1425/$ 9.95

Cookie Jars, Book II-Westfall-8½x11-256 Pgs.-(PB) ....#3440/$19.95

Debolt's Dictionary of American Pottery Marks-DeBolt-8½x11-288 Pgs.-(PB)................#3435/$17.95

Early Roseville-Huxford-5½x8½-72 Pgs.-(PB) ....#2076/$ 7.95

Head Vases-Cole-8½x11-142 Pgs.-(PB) ....#1917/$14.95

Lehner's Ency. of U.S. Marks on Pottery, Porcelain & Clay-Lehner-8½x11-644 Pgs.-(HB) ....#2379/$24.95

Purinton Pottery-Morris-8½x11-272 Pgs.-(HB) ....#3825/$24.95

Red Wing Stoneware-DePasquale-5½x8½-160 Pgs.-(PB) ....#1440/$ 9.95

Red Wing Collectibles-DePasquale-5½x8½-160 Pgs.-(PB) ....#1670/$ 9.95

Royal Copley-Wolfe-5½x8½-136 Pgs.-(PB) ....#2350/$14.95

More Royal Copley-Wolfe-5½x8½-128 Pgs.-(PB) ....#2351/$14.95

Shawnee Pottery-Mangus-8½x11-256 Pgs.-(HB) ....#3738/$24.95

Wall Pockets of the Past-Perkins-8½x11-160 Pgs.-(PB) ....#4572/$17.95

Watt Pottery Id. & Value Guide-Morris-8½x11-160 Pgs.-(HB) ....#3327/$19.95

This is only a partial listing of the books on pottery and porcelain that are available from Collector Books. All books are well illustrated and contain current values. Most of the following books are available from your local bookseller, antique dealer, or public library. If you are unable to locate certain titles in your area, you may order by mail from COLLECTOR BOOKS, P.O. Box 3009, Paducah, KY 42002-3009. Customers with Visa or MasterCard may phone in orders from 7:00–4:00 CST, Monday–Friday, Toll Free 1-800-626-5420. Add $2.00 for postage for the first book ordered and $0.30 for each additional book. Include item number, title, and price when ordering. Allow 14 to 21 days for delivery.

WE CARRY MORE THAN 300 BOOKS ON ANTIQUES & COLLECTIBLES • SEND FOR A FREE, COMPLETE LISTING OF ALL OUR TITLES

Schroeder's
ANTIQUES
Price Guide

. . . is the #1 best-selling antiques & collectibles value guide on the market today, and here's why . . .

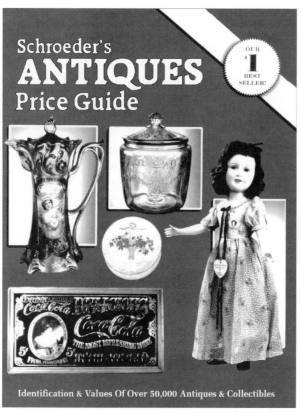

Schroeder's ANTIQUES Price Guide

OUR #1 BEST SELLER!

Identification & Values Of Over 50,000 Antiques & Collectibles

8½ x 11, 608 Pages, $14.95

• *More than 300 advisors, well-known dealers, and top-notch collectors work together with our editors to bring you accurate information regarding pricing and identification.*

• *More than 45,000 items in almost 500 categories are listed along with hundreds of sharp original photos that illustrate not only the rare and unusual, but the common, popular collectibles as well.*

• *Each large close-up shot shows important details clearly. Every subject is represented with histories and background information, a feature not found in any of our competitors' publications.*

• *Our editors keep abreast of newly developing trends, often adding several new categories a year as the need arises.*

If it merits the interest of today's collector, you'll find it in *Schroeder's*. And you can feel confident that the information we publish is up to date and accurate. Our advisors thoroughly check each category to spot inconsistencies, listings that may not be entirely reflective of market dealings, and lines too vague to be of merit. Only the best of the lot remains for publication.

Without doubt, you'll find
SCHROEDER'S ANTIQUES PRICE GUIDE
the only one to buy for
reliable information and values.

COLLECTOR BOOKS
A Division of Schroeder Publishing Co., Inc.